Fantastic Food from Your
MICRWAVE

151 TESTED RECIPES

Dr. GHAZI & BEVERLY TAKI
FOOD SCIENTIST   HOME ECONOMIST

Dedicated to you,
our valuable MICRO SHAKE customers
who want fantastic food from your microwave oven.

Acknowledgements:

Cover Book Design:	Campbell-Powell-Thompson-Baker Advertising, Inc.
Front Cover Photo:	George deGennaro
Back Cover Photo:	Wayne Wilcox Photography
Production:	Debra Warr
Typing/Proofreading:	Renee Shimer
Typography:	Malibu Typesetting
Printing:	Queens Group, Inc.
Production Manager:	Dr. Jeff Warr

ISBN: 0-9614957-0-7

Printed in the United States of America

First Printing: July 1985

TABLE OF CONTENTS

MEET THE AUTHORS

A common interest in microwave cooking brought this husband and wife team together. Beverly and Ghazi met at the test kitchen of a leading microwave oven manufacturer. Ghazi came to demonstrate his product, MICRO SHAKE, and there he met Beverly.

Beverly Gilliam Taki, a Home Economist, grew up in St. Louis and earned her B.S. degree from the University of Missouri in Columbia. She worked for five years as a Home Economist and Sales Training Specialist in microwave cooking. Since her marriage to Ghazi, she has been involved in every aspect of Microwave Foods, Inc. and MICRO SHAKE.

Dr. Ghazi Hussni Taki, Founder and President of Microwave Foods, Inc. and creator of MICRO SHAKE, has had a profound interest in microwave cooking since he earned his Ph.D. in 1965. Dr. Taki has been active in the food industry as a researcher, product developer, and consultant to a number of national and international companies. Throughout his professional career, he has dedicated himself to expanding the use and application of microwave ovens in food preparation as well as making microwave cooking more rewarding. Dr. Taki was born and raised in Baghdad, Iraq. He received his B.S. degree in Agriculture from the University of Baghdad. His M.S. degree in Meat Science was obtained at Oklahoma State University in 1961, and his Ph.D. from the University of Florida in Meat Science and Food Science.

"NOT JUST A MICROWAVE, BUT A WAY OF LIFE" . . . Dr. Taki

INTRODUCTION

You, the owner of a microwave oven have wanted fast, convenient, delicious and healthy food from your microwave oven. Your dream has come true! Here are 151 fantastic recipes designed, developed and tested by a Home Economist and Food Scientist that guarantee successful microwave cooking.

Fantastic Food from Your Microwave is full of interesting and fun recipes you can use every day, for any meal, and for any occasion. Every recipe was carefully developed to give you maximum nutrition with minimal preparation using common ingredients found in your kitchen. Each recipe was methodically tested and retested to make sure the results would be spectacular!

Fantastic Food from Your Microwave will help you master your microwave and enjoy better living with microwave cooking. It has it all -- from delicious appetizers to char-brown meats and golden-crusty chicken -- from impressive desserts to creative children's dishes.

Although every recipe in this book is delicious, we do have our favorites. The House Special at the beginning of each chapter are the recipes we use most frequently at home.

Note: The cooking time for these recipes is designed for 650 to 700 watt ovens. Since microwave ovens vary in rate of heating, cooking time is approximate and should be adjusted accordingly. So if your food is not cooked in the exact time given, give it another minute and relax!

THE STORY OF MICRO SHAKE

In 1976, Dr. Taki attended several microwave cooking classes and observed that most consumers were dissatisfied with the results of microwaved meat and poultry. In many of these classes the instructors offered a variety of solutions to the problems consumers faced when attempting to cook meats and poultry in a microwave. Most of these solutions were aimed at solving browning problems and most involved the use of available browning sauces, gravy or soup mixes. While some of these remedies were able to brown the meat, most were far from satisfactory. Usually, the microwaved meat was dry, tough and flavorless.

Dr. Taki spent years in graduate school researching meat and then many more years in the food industry managing research and product development. He set out to develop a product specifically designed to give meat and poultry cooked in the microwave the appearance and quality of conventionally cooked food.

After extensive research in the laboratory and a complete series of in-home tests, Dr. Taki introduced a pure food product that not only aided browning of meats and poultry, but also enhanced flavor and tenderness while sealing in juices. The product was named MICRO SHAKE and introduced to the market in 1977.

MICRO SHAKE MAKES THE DIFFERENCE

You will find that many of the recipes in this book will call for MICRO SHAKE as an important ingredient. MICRO SHAKE is an all-natural seasoning that solves the problems typically associated with cooking meats and poultry in microwave ovens. MICRO SHAKE browns, seasons, tenderizes, seals in natural juices and reduces shrinkage of meats and poultry. MICRO SHAKE does not contain sugar, monosodium glutamate (MSG), preservatives or artifical flavor. Salt Free MICRO SHAKE is available for those on sodium-restricted diets or for those who wish to limit their salt intake. MICRO SHAKE adds only a few calories per serving.

Original MICRO SHAKE comes in three flavors; Natural Meat Flavor, Onion & Garlic Flavor for Meat and Country Fried Chicken Flavor. Salt Free MICRO SHAKE is available in both Meat and Chicken Flavors. All MICRO SHAKE flavors are gourmet blends of spices, herbs, and other natural ingredients that will make microwave meat cookery a smashing success! The meat flavors are designed for beef, pork and lamb. The chicken flavors are designed for all poultry and wild game.

For recipes where MICRO SHAKE is used, please note that the meat flavors are interchangeable, as are the chicken flavors. Even though MICRO SHAKE was designed with microwave cooking in mind, it will give you the same benefits any way you cook; convection, barbecuing, frying, broiling, roasting and steaming. It also enhances flavor and browning when added to your favorite marinade.

MICRO SHAKE is available in microwave specialty stores, gourmet shops, and appliance and department stores. If you cannot find it in your favorite store, you can use the handy mail-order form at the back of this book.

A FAVORITE IN COOKING SCHOOLS NATIONWIDE!

VOLUNTARY CONSUMER TESTIMONIALS

"I think it is a great new product."
-Torrance, CA, 1977

"Gave up cooking in my microwave oven becuase I could not brown meats, but thanks to your product it's possible."
-Port Richley, FL, 1980

" . . . a miracle in overcoming the poor quality usually obtained in microwaved chicken and beef."
-Houston, TX, 1981

"It's the best thing that's happened since the microwave oven."
-Lake Hamilton, FL, 1981

"I want to thank you for MICRO SHAKE. Thank you for making it without preservatives, artificial color, sugar or MSG. It makes me happy to know that someone cares what people put in their bodies."
-Denver, CO, 1982

"I have been using your products for four (4) years and my family has really enjoyed them."
-Portsmouth, VA, 1983

"We like the char brown meat so much my 7 year old won't eat a hamburger made any other way."
-Slinger, WI, 1984

"A great big thanks to Dr. Taki for his MICRO SHAKE ideas because I have not been too successful with meats in my microwave. Now I'm really excited about trying meats again."
-Lockport, IL, 1985

Appetizers

Party Popcorn

4 tablespoons butter or margarine
1 tablespoon MICRO SHAKE - Chicken Flavor
2 to 3 quarts popped popcorn

1 . In a small bowl, place butter and MICRO SHAKE. Microwave on HIGH for 30 seconds or until melted. Mix well.

2 . Place popped popcorn in large serving bowl. Pour butter mixture over popcorn, tossing to coat evenly.

Yield: 2 to 3 quarts.

Bacon Popcorn

4 slices bacon
2 to 3 quarts popped popcorn

1 . Place bacon slices on a bacon rack. Microwave, covered with wax paper, on HIGH for 3 to 5 minutes or until crisp. Reserve drippings; crumble bacon.

2 . Place popped popcorn in a large serving bowl. Toss bacon with popcorn. Pour drippings over all, tossing to coat evenly.

Yield: 2 to 3 quarts.

Fantastic Almonds

2 tablespoons butter or margarine
4 teaspoons MICRO SHAKE - Chicken Flavor
1½ cups (8-ounces) whole, raw almonds, blanched

1 . In a small bowl, place butter and MICRO SHAKE. Microwave on HIGH for 30 seconds or until melted. Add almonds and stir until well coated.

2 . Microwave on HIGH for 7 minutes, stirring twice.

3 . Spread on paper towel-lined platter to cool before serving.

Yield: 1½ cups.

West Coast Nachos

1 package tortilla chips   1 can bean dip
1 jar salsa   Cheddar cheese, grated

1 . Place a layer of tortilla chips on a dinner plate. Spread salsa on top of chips. Mound bean dip on chips. Sprinkle with grated cheese.

2 . Microwave, covered, on HIGH for 2 minutes or until cheese is melted.

3 . Spread softened bean dip to cover all chips.

Serves 6 to 8.

Cheese Chili Dip

1 pound ground beef   ½ teaspoon cumin
1 cup onions, chopped   ¼ teaspoon oregano
1 tablespoon MICRO   leaves
   SHAKE - Meat Flavor   1 cup water
2 tablespoons flour   3 cups Cheddar cheese,
1 tablespoon chili   grated
   powder
2 jalapeno peppers,
   seeded and chopped

1 . In a colander with drip pan, place ground beef, onions and MICRO SHAKE. Microwave on HIGH for 5 to 6 minutes. Discard fat.

2 . In a 1½-quart casserole, combine meat mixture, flour chili powder, cumin, jalapeno peppers, oregano and water. Microwave on HIGH for 9 minutes. Stir cheese into hot mixture.

3 . Let stand 2 minutes before serving with tortilla chips.

Yield: 1 quart.

California Artichoke Dip

1 8½-ounce can artichoke hearts, chopped	1 tablespoon paprika
1 cup mayonnaise	1 tablespoon MICRO SHAKE - Chicken Flavor
1 cup Parmesan cheese, grated	

1 . In a 2-quart serving bowl, combine all ingredients. Stir well.

2 . Microwave, covered, on HIGH for 4 minutes. Stir well. Serve with crackers.

Serves 6 to 8.

Spinach Dip

1 10-ounce package frozen chopped spinach
1 8-ounce package cream cheese
1 cup sour cream
1 packet buttermilk dressing mix

1 . Puncture frozen carton of spinach 4 times with a fork. Place box on a plate. Microwave on MEDIUM for 3 minutes to defrost. Drain well.

2 . In a 1-quart casserole, place cream cheese. Microwave on HIGH for 45 seconds. Stir well.

3 . Add spinach, sour cream and buttermilk dressing packet to the cream cheese. Stir well.

4 . Serve with vegetables.

Serves 6 to 8.

Chip Beef Dip

1 8-ounce package
  cream cheese
½ cup sour cream
2 tablespoons cream
1 package dried
  chipped beef,
  chopped

2 tablespoons green
  pepper, chopped
2 tablespoons green
  onion, chopped
Dash Worcestershire
  sauce

1 . In a 1-quart casserole, place cream cheese. Microwave on HIGH for 45 seconds. Stir well.

2 . Add remaining ingredients. Stir. Microwave on MEDIUM HIGH for 5 to 6 minutes.

3 . Serve with corn chips.

Serves 6 to 8.

Classic Bacon Dip

1 8-ounce package
  cream cheese
1 cup sour cream
1 teaspoon instant
  minced onion

⅛ teaspoon garlic
  powder
5 strips bacon, cooked,
  crumbled
Paprika

1 . In a 1-quart casserole, place cream cheese. Microwave on HIGH for 45 seconds. Stir well.

2 . Add sour cream, minced onion, garlic powder and one-half of the crumbled bacon. Mix well.

3 . Microwave on MEDIUM HIGH for 4 to 5 minutes. Stir well.

4 . Sprinkle with paprika and remaining bacon bits.

5 . Serve with fresh vegetables or crackers.

Serves 6 to 8.

Appetizing Wings

6 chicken wings (12 pieces disjointed)
MICRO SHAKE - Chicken Flavor

1 . Cut chicken wings at joints into 3 parts; discard tip. Wash thoroughly. Sprinkle MICRO SHAKE liberally on all areas of chicken wings.

2 . On a round platter, place 12 chicken wings in a wagon-wheel formation, with meatiest portions towards outer edge of the dish. Sprinkle with MICRO SHAKE.

3 . Microwave, covered with wax paper, on HIGH for 6 to 8 minutes or until done.

4 . Let stand, covered, 3 minutes before serving. Garnish with sprigs of parsley and tomato wedges.

Yield: 12 appetizers.

Meatball Kabobs

1 pound ground beef, formed into 24 1-inch meatballs
MICRO SHAKE - Meat Flavor
1 small green pepper, cut into ¾ to 1-inch cubes

6 medium mushrooms, quartered
6 cherry tomatoes, cut in halves
½ small onion, cut into 1-inch cubes

1 . Prepare kabobs by placing a meatball in the center of a toothpick. On each side of the meatball, place one of the above vegetables. Make an assortment of kabobs with a variety of vegetables.

2 . Place twelve kabobs on a platter. Sprinkle each side of kabobs liberally with MICRO SHAKE.

3 . Microwave, covered with wax paper, on HIGH for 4 to 5 minutes or until done.

4 . Let stand, covered, 2 minutes before serving.

Yield: 24.

Italian Meatballs

1 pound lean ground beef
½ cup bread crumbs
1 teaspoon Italian seasoning
MICRO SHAKE - Meat Flavor

1 . Combine ground beef, bread crumbs and Italian seasoning. Form into 1-inch meatballs.

2 . Place meatballs in a shallow serving platter. Sprinkle
liberally with MICRO SHAKE to cover all surfaces.

3 . Microwave, covered, on HIGH for 5 to 6 minutes.

Yield: 24 meatballs.

Stuffed Mushrooms Italiano

12 medium-size fresh
mushrooms
MICRO SHAKE - Meat
Flavor
¼ pound lean ground
beef
2 tablespoons bread
crumbs

1 tablespoon Parmesan
cheese, grated
½ teaspoon Italian
seasoning
¼ teaspoon garlic
powder
Parsley flakes

1 . Wash mushrooms; cut small slice off end of stem and
discard. Remove and chop stems. Sprinkle MICRO
SHAKE into each mushroom cap; set aside.

2 . Combine one-half of chopped stems (save remainder for
use in soups, stews, etc.), ground beef, bread crumbs,
Parmesan cheese, Italian seasoning and garlic powder.
Mix well.

3 . Form mixture into 12 1-inch balls. Place a ball in each
mushroom cap. Place caps in a 2-quart baking dish leav-
ing some space between each cap. Sprinkle liberally with
MICRO SHAKE to cover all mushrooms. Top each with
parsley flakes.

4 . Microwave, covered, on HIGH for 2½ to 3 minutes.

Yield: 1 dozen.

Spinach Stuffed Mushrooms

1 tablespoon green
pepper, chopped
4 tablespoons onion,
chopped
1 tablespoon water
MICRO SHAKE - Meat
Flavor
1 pound ground beef
1 10-ounce package
frozen chopped
spinach

1 tomato, coarsely
chopped
1 teaspoon lemon juice
4 tablespoons Parmesan
cheese, grated
48 large mushroom
caps, stems
removed

1 . In a small bowl, place green pepper, onion, water and ½
teaspoon MICRO SHAKE. Microwave, covered, on HIGH
for 1 minute. Set aside.

2 . In a colander with drip pan, crumble ground beef.
Sprinkle with 1 tablespoon MICRO SHAKE. Microwave
on HIGH for 4 minutes.

3 . Cut spinach into 4 equal parts and place around outer
edge of colander containing meat. Microwave on HIGH
for 4 minutes.

4 . Chop spinach and mix well with hamburger. Add chopped tomato, onion mixture and lemon juice. Microwave
on HIGH for 2½ minutes.

5 . Sprinkle ¼ teaspoon Parmesan cheese into each
mushroom cap. Fill each cap with 1 tablespoon of the
above mixture. Sprinkle top with ⅛ teaspoon MICRO
SHAKE.

6 . Place 12 mushroom caps on a platter. Microwave,
covered with plastic wrap, on HIGH for 2 to 3 minutes.

7 . Let stand, covered, 1 minute.

Yield: 4 dozen.

Soups

Elegant Vegetable Soup

2 zucchini, cut into
   cubes
1 cup onion, chopped
4 ounces fresh
   mushrooms, sliced
4 tablespoons butter or
   margarine

2 tablespoons MICRO
   SHAKE - Chicken
   Flavor
¾ cup water
1 10¾-ounce can
   chicken broth
2 8-ounce packages
   cream cheese

1. In a 3-quart deep bowl, place vegetables, butter and MICRO SHAKE. Microwave, covered tightly, on HIGH for 10 minutes or until vegetables are tender, stirring once during cooking.

2. Add water and broth. Microwave, covered tightly, on HIGH for 10 minutes.

3. In a small bowl, place cream cheese. Microwave on HIGH for 1½ minutes to soften.

4. Add cream cheese to hot soup. Microwave, covered, on HIGH for 5 minutes. Stir well.

5. Let stand, covered, 2 minutes.

Serves 6 to 8.

Vegetable Beef Soup

1 pound lean ground
beef
½ cup onion, chopped
1 tablespoon MICRO
SHAKE - Meat Flavor
2 10¾-ounce cans
condensed beef noodle
soup

1½ soup cans water
1 10-ounce package
frozen peas and
carrots, thawed
1 8-ounce can tomatoes,
cut up

1 . In a colander with drip pan, crumble ground beef. Add
onions. Sprinkle with 1 tablespoon MICRO SHAKE.

2 . Microwave on HIGH for 5 minutes.

3 . In a 3-quart deep bowl, place meat. Add remaining ingredients. Stir well.

4 . Microwave, covered, on HIGH for 14 minutes. Stir.

5 . Let stand, covered, 2 minutes.

Serves 6 to 8.

Cream Cheese Onion Soup

2 cups onion, chopped
2 tablespoons butter or
margarine
2 tablespoons MICRO
SHAKE - Chicken
Flavor

¾ cup water
1 10¾-ounce can
chicken broth
2 8-ounce packages
cream cheese

1 . In a 3-quart deep bowl, place onions, butter and MICRO
SHAKE. Microwave, covered, on HIGH for 10 to 12 minutes
or until onions are tender, stirring once during cooking.

2 . Add water and broth. Microwave, covered, on HIGH for 10
minutes.

3 . In a small bowl, place cream cheese. Microwave on HIGH for
1½ minutes to soften.

4 . Add cream cheese to hot soup. Microwave, covered, on HIGH
for 3 to 5 minutes. Stir well.

5 . Let stand, covered, 2 minutes.

Serves 6 to 8.

Cream Of Broccoli Soup

¼ cup onion, chopped
2 tablespoons butter or
  margarine
1 teaspoon MICRO
  SHAKE - Chicken
  Flavor
1 10¾-ounce can
  condensed cream of
  celery soup

1 10¾-ounce can
  condensed cream of
  chicken soup
1 soup can milk
½ soup can water
1 10-ounce package
  frozen chopped
  broccoli, thawed

1 . In a small bowl, place onion, butter and MICRO SHAKE.
    Microwave, covered, on HIGH for 1 minute.

2 . In a 3-quart deep bowl, combine onions with remaining ingredients. Microwave, covered, on HIGH for 13 minutes. Stir.

3 . Let stand, covered, 2 minutes.

Serves 6 to 8.

Chicken Vegetable Noodle Soup

2 stalks celery, sliced
2 carrots, sliced
1 cup onion, chopped
¼ cup water
1 tablespoon MICRO
  SHAKE - Chicken
  Flavor

2 to 3 pounds chicken
  pieces
2 10¾-ounce cans
  condensed chicken
  broth & noodles soup
1½ soup cans water
1 tablespoon parsley
  flakes

1 . In a 3-quart deep bowl, place celery, carrots, onion, water and
    MICRO SHAKE. Microwave, covered tightly, on HIGH for 5
    minutes. Set aside.

2 . Moisten chicken pieces with water. Sprinkle each piece liberally with MICRO SHAKE to coat all surfaces. In a 2-quart baking
    dish, arrange chicken with meatiest pieces towards outer edge
    of dish. Microwave, covered, on HIGH for 8 minutes.

3 . Add soup and parsley flakes to vegetable mixture. Stir well.
    Add chicken pieces to vegetable mixture.

4 . Microwave, covered, on HIGH for 15 minutes.

5 . Let stand, covered, 5 minutes.

Serves 6 to 8.

Cook-Off Chili

6 tablespoons butter or margarine
MICRO SHAKE - Meat Flavor
⅔ pound chuck steak, cubed into 1-inch pieces after all fat and connective tissue have been removed
⅔ pound chuck steak, coarsely ground
1 large onion, chopped
1 green pepper, chopped
1 clove garlic, minced

3 tablespoons parsley, chopped
2 tablespoons chili powder
2 teaspoons salt
½ teaspoon black pepper
½ teaspoon cumin
¼ teaspoon coriander
1 16-ounce can tomatoes, including liquid
4 dashes hot sauce

1. In a 3-quart deep bowl, melt 3 tablespoons of butter or margarine on HIGH for 45 seconds. Add cubed steak and sprinkle liberally with MICRO SHAKE. Pierce meat with a fork. Microwave on MEDIUM HIGH for 5 minutes. Pour off 3 tablespoons of liquid.

2. In a colander with drip pan, place ground meat. Sprinkle liberally with MICRO SHAKE. Microwave on HIGH for 5 minutes.

3. In a 2-quart casserole combine onion, green pepper, garlic and parsley with 3 tablespoons of butter or margarine. Microwave, covered, on HIGH for 5 minutes.

4. Combine ground beef and vegetables with cubed meat in casserole. Stir in chili powder, salt, pepper, coriander and cumin. Add tomatoes and hot sauce.

5. Microwave, covered, on HIGH for 10 minutes.

6. Let stand, covered, 5 minutes.

Serves 4.

Simple To Do Chili

1½ pounds lean ground
 beef
1 large onion, chopped
1 green pepper, diced
2 stalks celery, chopped
MICRO SHAKE - Meat
 Flavor

1 teaspoon chili powder
1 16-ounce can kidney
 beans
3 16-ounce cans tomato
 sauce

1 . In a 3-quart deep bowl, combine ground beef, onion, green pepper and celery. Sprinkle liberally with MICRO SHAKE.

2 . Microwave on HIGH for 8 to 10 minutes. Stir well to break up meat. Drain off grease.

3 . Add chili powder, beans and tomato sauce. Stir well.

4 . Microwave on MEDIUM for 25 minutes. Stir well.

5 . Let stand, covered, 5 minutes.

Serves 4.

Potato Cheese Chowder

3 large potatoes, peeled
 and thinly sliced
1 large carrot, sliced
1 stalk celery, sliced
¼ cup onion, chopped
1 cup water
1 chicken bouillon cube

⅛ teaspoon pepper
2 tablespoons flour
1 cup milk
1 8-ounce package
 processed cheese
 spread

1 . In a 3-quart deep bowl, combine vegetables, water, bouillon and pepper. Microwave, covered, on HIGH for 12 to 14 minutes or until vegetables are tender.

2 . In a small bowl, gradually add flour to milk. Add flour mixture to vegetables. Mix well.

3 . Microwave on HIGH for 7 minutes or until thickened.

4 . Add cheese. Microwave on HIGH for 2 minutes or until cheese is melted.

5 . Let stand 2 minutes.

Serves 4.

New England Clam Chowder

5 slices bacon	2 tablespoons flour
1 8-ounce can minced clams	1 ½ cups milk
2 potatoes, peeled and cubed	1 cup cream
1 small onion, finely chopped	1 teaspoon salt
	½ teaspoon pepper

1 . In a 3-quart deep bowl, place bacon. Microwave, covered, on HIGH for 4 minutes or until bacon is crisp. Remove cooked bacon, crumble and set aside. Reserve drippings in bowl.

2 . Drain clams and add liquid to bacon drippings. Rinse clams and set aside.

3 . Add potatoes and onions to liquid. Microwave, covered, on HIGH for 9 minutes or until vegetables are tender.

4 . Blend flour into mixture. Gradually stir in milk until smooth.

5 . Microwave on HIGH for 7 minutes or until thickened and smooth. Stir well.

6 . Stir in cream, salt, pepper and clams. Microwave on HIGH for 4 minutes. Stir.

7 . Let stand, covered, 2 minutes.

8 . Serve garnished with crumbled bacon.

Serves 4.

NOTES _____
_____
_____
_____
_____
_____

Meat

Malibu Burger Steak

1 pound lean ground
   beef
MICRO SHAKE - Meat
   Flavor
1 onion, thinly
   sliced

1 large tomato, sliced
10 mushrooms, sliced
1 green pepper, cut
   into rings

1 . In a 2-quart serving dish, place four slices onion, top with four slices tomato.

2 . Shape ground beef into four patties. Moisten both sides of each patty with water. Sprinkle each side liberally with MICRO SHAKE and place on top of tomato.

3 . Place mushroom slice and ring of green pepper on top of each beef patty.

4 . Coarsely chop remaining vegetables and place around patties. Sprinkle MICRO SHAKE liberally over vegetables.

5 . Microwave, covered with wax paper, on HIGH for 9 to 11 minutes or until meat is desired degree of doneness.

6 . Let stand, covered, 3 minutes.

Serves 4.

Beef Florentine

1 tablespoon green
pepper, chopped
4 tablespoons onion,
chopped
1 tablespoon water
MICRO SHAKE - Meat
Flavor
1 pound ground
beef

1 10-ounce package
frozen chopped
spinach
1 tomato, coarsely
chopped
1 teaspoon lemon juice
4 tablespoons Parmesan
cheese, grated

1 . In a small bowl, place green pepper, onion, water and ½ teaspoon MICRO SHAKE. Microwave, covered, on HIGH for 1
minute. Set aside.

2 . In a colander with drip pan, crumble ground beef. Sprinkle
with 1 tablespoon MICRO SHAKE. Microwave on HIGH for 4
minutes. Stir to break up.

3 . Cut spinach into 4 equal parts and place around outer edge of
colander containing meat. Microwave on HIGH for 4 minutes.

4 . In a 2-quart casserole, place spinach and hamburger. Mix well.
Add chopped tomato, onion mixture and lemon juice.
Microwave on HIGH for 2½ minutes.

5 . Serve over seasoned rice below.

Serves 4.

Seasoned Rice

1½ cups water
2½ teaspoons MICRO
SHAKE - Meat
Flavor

2 teaspoons butter or
margarine
1½ cups packaged pre-
cooked rice

1 . In a 1-quart casserole combine water, MICRO SHAKE and butter.

2 . Microwave on HIGH for 5 minutes or until it reaches a full
boil.

3 . Stir in rice. Microwave on HIGH for 15 to 20 seconds just to
heat.

4 . Let stand, covered with plastic wrap, 5 minutes.

Serves 4.

Beef With Spinach & Noodles

1 pound ground beef
2 tablespoons MICRO
   SHAKE - Meat Flavor
1 10-ounce package
   frozen chopped
   spinach
1 4-ounce can mushroom
   pieces, drained

1 10¾-ounce can
   condensed cream of
   mushroom soup
1 cup small curd cottage
   cheese
2 cups cooked wide egg
   noodles
1 3-ounce can french
   fried onions

1 . In a colander with drip pan, crumble ground beef. Sprinkle
    with 1 tablespoon MICRO SHAKE. Microwave on HIGH for 5
    minutes. Stir to break up.

2 . Puncture frozen carton of spinach 4 times with a fork. Place
    box on a plate. Microwave on HIGH for 5 minutes. Drain
    well.

3 . In a 2-quart serving bowl, combine hamburger, spinach,
    mushroom pieces, soup, cottage cheese and 1 tablespoon
    MICRO SHAKE. Add noodles and one-half of onions.

4 . Microwave on HIGH for 5 minutes. Stir well.

5 . Sprinkle remaining onions on top. Microwave on HIGH
    for 5 minutes or until heated through.

Noodles

1 . In a 2-quart mixing bowl, place 2 cups water and 1 tea-
    spoon vegetable oil. Microwave on HIGH for 5 to 6
    minutes or until boiling.

2 . Add 2 cups of wide egg noodles. Microwave, covered tightly,
    on HIGH for 6 minutes.

3 . Let stand, covered, for 10 minutes. Drain well.

Serves 6.

Meatloaf

1½ pounds lean ground
  beef
1 cup bread crumbs
1 small onion, finely
  chopped
1 egg, slightly beaten

¼ cup catsup
1 teaspoon prepared
  mustard
MICRO SHAKE - Meat
  Flavor

1 . In a large bowl, combine all ingredients except MICRO
    SHAKE. Blend well.

2 . Shape meat mixture into loaf dish, 6-cup ring mold or shape
    into individual mini-loaves and arrange on a roasting rack.

3 . Sprinkle MICRO SHAKE over top of meat.

4 . Microwave, covered with wax paper, on HIGH for 14 to 18
    minutes for loaf shape. Microwave on HIGH for 10 to 14
    minutes for ring shape or individual mini-loaves or until meat
    thermometer registers 145° Fahrenheit.

5 . Let stand, covered with wax paper, 3 to 5 minutes.

Serves 4 to 6.

Roast Beef

5 to 6 pound standing rib roast, well trimmed
Red wine or water
MICRO SHAKE - Meat Flavor

1 . Moisten meat with red wine or water. Sprinkle each side
    liberally with MICRO SHAKE. Pierce meat on all sides with a
    fork at ½-inch intervals.

2 . On a roasting rack, place roast, fat side down. Microwave on
    HIGH for 14 to 16 minutes (5½ minutes per pound for rare;
    6½ minutes per pound for medium).

3 . Turn meat over; may desire to baste meat with drippings.
    Microwave on HIGH for 14 to 16 minutes.

4 . Let stand, covered, for 10 to 15 minutes or until meat ther-
    mometer registers 140°F to 150°F rare; 160°F medium; 170°F
    well done.

Serves 6 to 8.

Fruited Pot Roast
(Clay Pot Cooking)

½ cup prunes
½ cup dried apricots
3 medium potatoes,
  peeled and cut into
  bite-size pieces
½ onion, cut into
  wedges
1 cup beer
MICRO SHAKE - Meat
  Flavor

¼ teaspoon cinnamon
2 tablespoons honey
1½ tablespoons brown
  sugar
⅛ teaspoon ground
  ginger
2 pounds boneless chuck
  pot roast
2 tablespoons cornstarch
¼ cup water

1. Pre-soak clay pot 10 minutes.

2. Place fruit and vegetables in clay pot. In a small bowl, combine ¾ cup beer, ½ teaspoon MICRO SHAKE, cinnamon, honey, brown sugar and ginger. Pour over fruits and vegetables.

3. Microwave on HIGH for 5 minutes.

4. Moisten meat with remaining beer. Sprinkle liberally with MICRO SHAKE to coat all surfaces. Pierce meat with a fork at ½-inch intervals. Place meat on top of vegetables.

5. Microwave, covered, on HIGH for 5 minutes. Reduce power to MEDIUM and continue to microwave for 20 minutes.

6. Turn meat over and stir vegetables and fruit. Microwave, covered, on MEDIUM for 20 to 30 minutes or until meat and vegetables are fork tender.

7. Remove meat, fruit and vegetables to serving platter with a slotted spoon; keep warm.

8. Combine cornstarch and water. Stir to make a smooth mixture. Whisk into meat juices. Microwave on HIGH for 2 to 4 minutes or until desired thickness, stirring twice. Serve with meat, fruit and vegetables.

Serves 4 to 6.

Traditional Pot Roast

2½ to 3 pounds beef
   chuck roast
MICRO SHAKE - Meat
   Flavor
1 cup water, wine or
   broth

4 carrots, cut into
   1½-inch strips
2 large potatoes, peeled
   and cut into quarters
2 onions, cut into eighths

1 . Moisten both sides of meat with water. Sprinkle liberally with
MICRO SHAKE. Pierce meat with a fork at ½-inch intervals.

2 . In a 3-quart deep bowl, place meat and desired liquid.

3 . Microwave, covered, on HIGH for 5 minutes.

4 . Reduce power to MEDIUM and continue to microwave,
covered, for 25 minutes.

5 . Turn meat over and arrange vegetables around meat.
Microwave, covered, on MEDIUM for an additional 25 to 35
minutes or until meat and vegetables are fork tender.

6 . Let stand, covered, 5 minutes.

Serves 4.

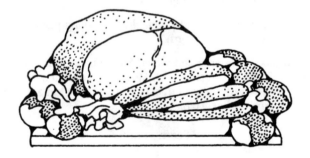

"Old Fashioned" Stew

1 pound chuck steak, cut
  into 1-inch cubes
MICRO SHAKE - Meat
  Flavor
1 stalk celery, cut into
  1-inch pieces
2 carrots, cut into 1-inch
  pieces

1 potato, pared and
  cubed
1 small onion, cut into
  eighths
1 cup red wine, beer,
  tomato juice or water

1. Moisten meat with water or wine.

2. In a 3-quart deep casserole, place meat cubes. Sprinkle 1½ teaspoons MICRO SHAKE on meat. Pierce with a fork. Microwave, covered, on HIGH for 3 minutes.

3. Add vegetables to meat. Sprinkle 1½ teaspoons MICRO SHAKE to cover all vegetables. Add 1 cup red wine or liquid. Mix well. Microwave, covered, on HIGH for 15 to 17 minutes. Stir twice during cooking.

4. Let stand, covered, 5 minutes.

Serves 2.

NOTES _____

_____

_____

_____

_____

_____

_____

_____

_____

Steak With Pepper Sauce

2 lean boneless steaks, ½ to ¾-inch thick
(4 to 6 ounces each)
MICRO SHAKE - Meat Flavor

Sauce

2 tablespoons butter or margarine
½ teaspoon Worcester-shire sauce

1 tablespoon lemon juice
½ teaspoon coarsely crushed black pepper

1 . Moisten both sides of each steak with water. Sprinkle each side liberally with MICRO SHAKE. Pierce meat on both sides with a fork.

2 . In a shallow baking dish, place steaks.

3 . Microwave on HIGH for 7 to 8 minutes or until desired degree of doneness.

4 . Let stand, covered, 1 minute.

5 . In a small bowl, combine sauce ingredients. Microwave on HIGH for 45 to 60 seconds. Stir and pour over steaks.

Serves 2.

Beef and Vegetable Platter

1 pound round steak, ¾
  to 1-inch thick, cut
  into 1-inch cubes
MICRO SHAKE - Meat
  Flavor
1 green pepper, cut into
  ¾ to 1-inch cubes

½ medium onion, cut
  into 1-inch cubes
6 medium mushrooms,
  quartered
6 cherry tomatoes, cut
  in halves

1 . Moisten meat with water or red wine. Sprinkle liberally with MICRO SHAKE. Pierce meat with a fork.

2 . On a 12-inch round platter, arrange green pepper cubes in a circle around outer edge of platter. Place meat cubes next to peppers, then onions and mushrooms. End with tomatoes piled in center.

3 . Sprinkle MICRO SHAKE liberally over vegetables and meat.

4 . Microwave, covered, on MEDIUM HIGH for 12 to 13 minutes or until meat is desired degree of doneness.

5 . Let stand, covered, 2 minutes before serving over a bed of rice or as appetizers.

Serves 4.

Flank Steak with Southern Stuffing
(Clay Pot Cooking)

4 green onions, chopped
1 small clove garlic,
   minced
1 tablespoon olive oil
4 ounces pork sausage,
   crumbled
1½ teaspoons chili
   powder
⅛ teaspoon oregano

1 cup corn bread stuffing
¼ cup fresh parsley,
   chopped
MICRO SHAKE - Meat
   Flavor
1½ to 2 pounds flank or
   round steak
¼ cup red wine or
   water

1 . Pre-soak clay pot 10 minutes.

2 . Place onion, garlic and olive oil in clay pot. Microwave on HIGH for 1½ to 2 minutes or until tender. Add sausage, chili powder, oregano, corn bread stuffing, parsley and ½ teaspoon MICRO SHAKE. Mix well.

3 . Spread stuffing on flank steak. Roll up like a jelly roll. Secure with wooden picks or tie with string every 1½ inches.

4 . Place meat, seam side up in clay pot. Pour ¼ cup wine or water over meat to moisten. Sprinkle liberally with MICRO SHAKE. Pierce meat with a fork at ½-inch intervals.

5 . Microwave, covered, on HIGH for 5 minutes. Reduce power to MEDIUM and continue to microwave for 10 minutes.

6 . Turn meat over. Spoon some pan juices over meat and sprinkle with MICRO SHAKE.

7 . Microwave, covered, on MEDIUM for 30 to 40 minutes or until meat is tender. Spoon juices over meat.

Serves 4 to 6.

Beef 'n Rice Provencale
(Clay Pot Cooking)

1 cup long grain white
   rice, uncooked
1 onion, finely chopped
1 clove garlic, minced
¼ teaspoon thyme
1 crumbled bay leaf
⅛ teaspoon saffron
   (optional)
1½ cups tomato puree

⅓ cup dry white wine
⅔ cup water
2 pounds chuck steak,
   cut into ½-inch cubes
1½ teaspoons MICRO
   SHAKE - Meat Flavor
1 cup Swiss cheese,
   grated

1. Pre-soak clay pot 10 minutes.

2. Place rice, onion, garlic, thyme, bay leaf and saffron in clay pot.

3. In a small bowl, combine tomato puree, wine and water. Stir into rice mixture.

4. Moisten meat with water. Sprinkle liberally with MICRO SHAKE. Pierce meat with a fork. Place beef cubes over rice.

5. Microwave, covered, on HIGH for 5 minutes. Reduce to MEDIUM and continue to microwave for 10 minutes. Stir well.

6. Microwave on MEDIUM an additional 20 to 30 minutes or until beef is tender, stirring halfway. Add Swiss cheese. Stir well.

Serves 4 to 6.

NOTES

Pepper Steak Strips

1 ½ pounds boneless beef
round steak, ½-inch
thick
MICRO SHAKE - Meat
Flavor
¼ cup teriyaki sauce
2 tablespoons butter or
margarine
1 medium green pepper,
cut into thin strips
2 celery stalks, thinly
sliced

1 clove garlic, minced or
pressed
¼ cup water
1 cup green onion,
chopped
2 medium tomatoes,
peeled and cut into
chunks
2 cups long grain rice,
cooked

1. Trim fat from meat and cut into ¼-inch wide strips. Moisten
   meat with water. Sprinkle liberally with MICRO SHAKE. Pierce
   meat with a fork.

2. In a 2-quart baking dish, place meat. Add teriyaki sauce and
   butter.

3. Microwave, covered, on HIGH for 5 to 6 minutes or until
   brown. Stir.

4. Add onion, celery, garlic and water.

5. Microwave on MEDIUM for 11 to 14 minutes or until
   vegetables are tender. Add green pepper and tomato. Stir well.

6. Microwave on HIGH for 2½ to 4 minutes.

7. Let stand, covered, 5 minutes.

Serves 4.

Pot Roast
(Clay Pot Cooking)

3 to 4 pounds pork loin
  roast
Lemon juice
MICRO SHAKE - Meat
  Flavor
1 pound large mushroom
  caps

½ teaspoon freshly
  ground pepper
3 medium apples, cored
  and quartered
¼ cup sugar, combined
  with ½ teaspoon
  cinnamon

1. Pre-soak clay pot 10 minutes.

2. Place roast in clay pot fat side down. Moisten with lemon juice. Sprinkle liberally with MICRO SHAKE. Pierce roast with a fork at ½-inch intervals.

3. Cover with clay lid. Microwave on HIGH for 15 to 20 minutes (5 minutes per pound).

4. Turn roast over; sprinkle liberally with MICRO SHAKE. Microwave, covered, on MEDIUM for 30 minutes.

5. Sprinkle inside of mushroom caps with pepper. Place on roast. Dip cut sides of apples in lemon juice, then toss in cinnamon-sugar mixture. Arrange apples around roast.

6. Continue to microwave, covered, on MEDIUM for 20 to 30 minutes or until roast, mushrooms and apples are tender. Baste with juices.

7. Let stand, covered, 10 to 15 minutes or until meat thermometer registers 170° Fahrenheit. Slice roast and spoon juices over top.

Serves 4.

Applesauce

6 to 8 medium cooking
   apples, cored, pared
   and quartered
½ cup water

⅓ cup sugar
1 teaspoon lemon juice
½ teaspoon cinnamon
¼ teaspoon nutmeg

1. In a 3-quart deep casserole, place apples and water.

2. Microwave, covered, on HIGH for 8 minutes or until apples are tender.

3. Add sugar. Mash apples. Add lemon juice.

4. Add cinnamon and nutmeg. Stir well.

Fruit Stuffed Pork Loin Roast

3 to 4 pound boneless
   pork loin roast
Moist-pack assorted dried
   fruit (apricots, prunes,
   apples, peaches)

MICRO SHAKE - Meat
   Flavor
Water, white wine or
   apple juice

1. Cut a pocket into each end of roast, all the way through. Stuff pocket with dried fuits.

2. Moisten roast with water, wine or apple juice. Sprinkle each side liberally with MICRO SHAKE. Pierce meat on all sides with a fork at ½-inch intervals.

3. On a roasting rack, place roast fat side down.

4. Microwave, covered, on HIGH for 5 minutes. Reduce power to MEDIUM HIGH and microwave 12 to 14 minutes per pound. Turn roast over halfway through cooking time. Drain excess juices periodically.

5. When completely cooked, roast should register 170° Fahrenheit with a meat thermometer.

6. Let stand, tented with foil, 5 minutes.

Serves 5 to 6.

Lazy Man's Barbecued Chops

2 pork chops, ¾ to
1-inch thick
MICRO SHAKE - Meat
Flavor
1 16-ounce can pork and
beans
4 medium mushrooms,
sliced
2 tablespoons onion,
chopped

1 tablespoon green
pepper, chopped
1 tablespoon catsup
1 teaspoon prepared
mustard
1 teaspoon Worcester-
shire sauce
3 dashes Tabasco

1 . Trim excess fat and slit remaining fat on pork chops.

2 . Moisten both sides of each chop with water. Sprinkle each
side liberally with MICRO SHAKE. Pierce meat on both sides
with a fork.

3 . In a 1½-quart shallow casserole, combine pork and beans
with remaining ingredients. Mix well.

4 . Place pork chops on bean mixture with bones toward outer
edge of dish.

5 . Microwave, covered, on MEDIUM for 18 minutes or until
meat is done.

6 . Let stand, covered, 3 minutes.

Serves 2.

Iowa Barbecued Chops

2 pork chops, ¾ to 1-inch thick
MICRO SHAKE - Meat Flavor

Sauce

½ cup catsup
1 tablespoon lemon
   juice
1 tablespoon vinegar
1 tablespoon Worcester-
   shire sauce

2 tablespoons onion,
   finely chopped
2 tablespoons celery,
   chopped
2 tablespoons brown
   sugar
1 teaspoon orange peel,
   finely grated

1 . Trim excess fat and slit remaining fat on pork chops.

2 . Moisten both sides of each chop with water. Sprinkle each
side liberally with MICRO SHAKE. Pierce meat on both sides
with a fork.

3 . In a shallow baking dish, arrange pork chops with bones
toward outer edge of dish.

4 . Microwave, covered, on HIGH for 4 minutes.

5 . In a small bowl, combine sauce ingredients. Mix well.

6 . Turn pork chops over and cover with one-half of sauce and
continue microwaving for 4 minutes or until chops are done.

7 . Pour accumulated sauce from dish into a small bowl with remaining sauce. Microwave on HIGH for 5 to 7 minutes or
until thickened. Pour over chops.

Serves 2.

Pork Chops With Sauerkraut

**1 26-ounce can sauerkraut, well drained
4 pork chops, ¾ to 1-inch thick
MICRO SHAKE - Meat Flavor**

1 . In a shallow baking dish, spread sauerkraut evenly.

2 . Trim excess fat and slit remaining fat on pork chops.

3 . Moisten both sides of each chop with water. Sprinkle each side liberally with MICRO SHAKE. Pierce meat on both sides with a fork.

4 . Place pork chops on sauerkraut with bones toward outer edge of dish.

5 . Microwave, covered, on HIGH for 5 minutes. Reduce to MEDIUM and microwave for 18 to 22 minutes or until meat is done.

6 . Let stand, covered, 3 minutes.

Serves 4.

Stuffed Pork Chops

**4 pork chops, 1-inch thick, pockets cut
2 cups bread or cornbread stuffing
MICRO SHAKE - Meat Flavor**

1 . Fill pockets of pork chops with your favorite bread stuffing. Secure openings with wooden picks.

2 . Moisten both sides of each chop with water. Sprinkle each side liberally with MICRO SHAKE. Pierce meat on both sides with a fork.

3 . In a 2-quart shallow baking dish, arrange chops with bones toward outer edge of dish.

4 . Microwave, covered, on MEDIUM for 25 to 30 minutes or until done.

5 . Let stand, covered, 3 minutes.

Serves 4.

Greek Lamb Chops

1 cup onion, chopped
2 tablespoons olive or
  vegetable oil
4 lamb chops (about 2
  pounds)
MICRO SHAKE - Meat
  Flavor
1 16-ounce can cut green
  beans, drained

1 16-ounce can whole,
  peeled tomatoes
1 2¼-ounce can black
  olives, sliced
2 tablespoons Worcester-
  shire sauce
1 teaspoon parsley flakes

1. In a medium bowl, place onion and 1 tablespoon olive oil.
   Microwave on HIGH for 3 minutes or until tender.

2. Trim excess fat from lamb chops. Moisten both sides of each
   chop with 1 tablespoon olive oil. Sprinkle each side liberally
   with MICRO SHAKE. Pierce meat on both sides with a fork.

3. In a shallow baking dish, place chops with bones toward outer
   edge of dish. Microwave, covered, on MEDIUM for 10
   minutes.

4. Add remaining ingredients to onion mixture. Stir well.
   Distribute evenly over cooked lamb chops.

5. Microwave, covered, on HIGH for 10 minutes or until
   vegetables are done.

6. Let stand, covered, 3 minutes.

Serves 4.

NOTES _____

_____

_____

_____

_____

_____

_____

Lamb Roast
(Clay Pot Cooking)

4 medium carrots, cut in
   thin strips
2 medium potatoes, cut
   in bite-size chunks
1 small eggplant, cut into
   ½-inch cubes
4 pearl onions
2 cloves garlic, minced
2 medium zucchini,
   sliced ½-inch thick
2 tablespoons celery
   tops, finely chopped

1 8-ounce can stewed
   tomatoes
1 tablespoon fresh
   parsley, chopped
½ teaspoon allspice
½ teaspoon coriander
1 bay leaf
MICRO SHAKE - Meat
   Flavor
2 to 3 pounds lamb
   shoulder roast

1. Pre-soak clay pot 10 minutes.

2. Place vegetables, except tomatoes, with herbs and spices in
   clay pot. Sprinkle 1½ teaspoons MICRO SHAKE over
   vegetables. Pour tomatoes over all.

3. Microwave, covered, on HIGH for 8 minutes. Stir.

4. Moisten meat with water. Sprinkle liberally with MICRO
   SHAKE to coat all surfaces. Pierce meat with a fork at ½-inch
   intervals. Place meat on top of vegetables.

5. Microwave, covered, on HIGH for 5 minutes. Reduce power
   to MEDIUM and continue to microwave for 25 minutes.

6. Turn meat over. Rearrange vegetables. Microwave, covered,
   on MEDIUM for 35 to 40 minutes or until meat and vegetables
   are fork tender.

Serves 4 to 6.

Venison with Vegetables & Wine

2 pounds venison or lean
   beef stew meat, cut
   into 1-inch cubes
MICRO SHAKE - Meat
   Flavor
2 medium onions,
   quartered
2 cloves garlic, minced
¼ teaspoon allspice
1 bay leaf
⅛ teaspoon pepper

1 beef bouillon cube
2 cups hot water
¼ cup marsala wine
2 carrots, thinly sliced
1 zucchini, thinly sliced
1 cup dried apricots,
   diced
¼ cup flour

1 .   In a 2-quart casserole, place meat cubes. Sprinkle 3 teaspoons
MICRO SHAKE on meat. Pierce meat with a fork. Add onion,
garlic, allspice, bay leaf and pepper.

2 .   Dissolve bouillon cube in hot water. Add water and wine to
meat.

3 .   Microwave, covered, on HIGH for 8 minutes.

4 .   Add carrots, zucchini and apricots. Stir. Microwave, covered,
on MEDIUM for 30 minutes, stirring after 15 minutes.

5 .   Remove 1 cup broth and blend in flour until smooth. Add
back to meat and vegetable mixture. Stir.

6 .   Microwave on HIGH for 1 to 2 minutes or until sauce has
thickened slightly.

Serves 4.

Poultry

Low Calorie Savory Chicken

2½ to 3 pounds
  chicken parts, skin
  removed
¼ cup lemon juice,
  white wine or water
MICRO SHAKE -
  Chicken Flavor

1 cup finely sliced
  carrots, celery,
  zucchini combination
1 small onion, sliced
¼ pound fresh or 4-
  ounce can
  mushrooms, sliced

1 . In a 2-quart baking dish, place vegetables. Sprinkle with
    1 teaspoon MICRO SHAKE.

2 . Moisten chicken pieces with lemon juice, wine or water.
    Sprinkle each piece liberally with MICRO SHAKE to coat
    all surfaces. Arrange chicken over vegetables with
    meatiest pieces towards outer edge of dish.

3 . Add remaining liquid to vegetables. Microwave, covered
    with wax paper, on HIGH for 16 to 18 minutes or until
    done.

4 . Let stand, covered, 5 minutes.

Serves 4.

Stuffed Chicken A La Micro Shake

3 to 4 pound chicken
Prepared package stuffing mix or your favorite bread
stuffing
MICRO SHAKE - Chicken Flavor

1 . Wash chicken. Sprinkle cavity of chicken with MICRO SHAKE. Stuff.

2 . Secure openings with wooden picks and tie legs.

3 . Moisten chicken with water. Sprinkle liberally with MICRO SHAKE to coat all sides.

4 . Place chicken breast side down on a roasting rack.

5 . Calculate total cooking time by using 8 minutes per pound. Microwave, covered with wax paper, on HIGH for one-half the total cooking time.

6 . Turn breast side up. Sprinkle with MICRO SHAKE. Baste with drippings.

7 . Microwave, covered, for second half of calculated cooking time or until internal temperature of meatiest area is 170° Fahrenheit with a meat thermometer. Baste with drippings.

8 . Let stand, tented with foil, 5 to 10 minutes before carving.

Serves 4.

Country Chicken 'n Rice

1½ cups packaged pre-
cooked rice
½ green pepper, finely
chopped
½ onion, finely chopped
1 16-ounce can garbanzo
beans, drained
¾ teaspoon Italian
seasoning, or ½
teaspoon oregano

1 clove garlic, crushed
1 8-ounce can stewed
tomatoes
¼ cup water
2½ to 3 pounds chicken
parts
MICRO SHAKE - Chicken
Flavor

1 . In a 2-quart shallow baking dish, place rice. Place pepper,
onion, garbanzo beans and Italian seasoning over rice.

2 . Stir crushed garlic into can of stewed tomatoes and pour over
rice . Add water to mixture. Sprinkle with MICRO SHAKE.

3 . Moisten chicken pieces with water. Sprinkle liberally with
MICRO SHAKE to coat all surfaces. Place chicken over
vegetables with meatiest pieces towards outer edge of dish.

4 . Microwave, covered, on HIGH for 5 minutes. Reduce power
to MEDIUM HIGH and microwave for 30 to 35 minutes or
until fork tender.

5 . Let stand, covered, 10 minutes.

Serves 4 to 6.

Chicken 'n Cornbread

1 onion, finely chopped
1 cup celery, finely
  chopped
MICRO SHAKE - Chicken
  Flavor
1 6½-ounce package
  cornbread stuffing

1 2-ounce jar pimiento,
  chopped
1 10¾-ounce can
  condensed cream of
  mushroom soup
1 cup water
2½ to 3 pounds chicken
  parts

1 . In a 2-quart oblong baking dish, combine celery, onion and
    1½ teaspoons MICRO SHAKE. Microwave, covered, on HIGH
    for 2 to 3 minutes or until tender. Add cornbread stuffing and
    pimiento.

2 . In a small bowl, combine soup and water. Add to stuffing
    mixture. Pat mixture into baking dish.

3 . Moisten chicken pieces with water. Sprinkle liberally with
    MICRO SHAKE to coat all surfaces. Arrange chicken pieces on
    stuffing mixture, placing meatiest pieces towards outer edge of
    dish.

4 . Microwave, covered, on HIGH for 17 to 21 minutes or until
    done.

5 . Let stand, covered, 5 minutes.

Serves 4.

Chicken with Artichoke Hearts

2½ to 3 pounds chicken parts
MICRO SHAKE - Chicken Flavor
¼ teaspoon garlic powder
¼ teaspoon oregano leaves

¾ cup white wine
1 bunch green onions, chopped
½ pound mushrooms, sliced
2 6-ounce jars marinated artichoke hearts

1. Moisten chicken pieces with water or white wine. Sprinkle each piece liberally with MICRO SHAKE to coat all surfaces.

2. In a 2-quart oblong baking dish, mix garlic, oregano and wine. Arrange pieces of chicken in baking dish with meatiest pieces towards outer edge of dish. Place green onions, mushrooms, and artichoke hearts around (not over) chicken.

3. Microwave, covered, on HIGH for 20 to 25 minutes or until done.

4. Let stand, covered, 5 minutes before serving with rice or noodles.

Serves 4.

Chicken Breast with Cheese and Herbs

2 tablespoons butter or margarine
½ cup sharp Cheddar cold pack cheese food
1½ teaspoons chives

⅛ teaspoon each of dill weed, thyme, rosemary and tarragon
4 whole chicken breasts, halved, boned and skin removed
MICRO SHAKE - Chicken Flavor

1. In a small bowl, place butter and cheese. Microwave on HIGH for 30 seconds to soften.

2. Add chives and spices. Mix well.

3. Pound chicken breasts with flat side of meat mallet to ¼-inch thickness.

4. Place about 1½ tablespoons of cheese mixture on each flattened piece.

5. Roll breasts, secure openings with wooden pick.

6. Moisten outer sides of each roll with water. Sprinkle liberally with MICRO SHAKE to coat all surfaces.

7. In a shallow baking dish, place breasts. Microwave, covered, on HIGH for 8 to 10 minutes. Serve with wine sauce below.

Serves 4 to 6.

Wine Sauce
2 tablespoons butter or margarine
2 tablespoons white wine
Pinch each parsley, marjoram and oregano

1. In a small bowl, place butter. Microwave on HIGH for 30 seconds. Add remaining ingredients. Stir well.

Chinese Chicken and Vegetables

3 chicken breasts,
skinned, boned, and
cut in 1-inch pieces
MICRO SHAKE - Chicken
Flavor
1 cup celery, diagonally
sliced
1 16-ounce can Chinese
vegetables, drained
1 16-ounce can bean
sprouts, drained
1 8-ounce can water
chestnuts, drained
and thinly sliced

2 to 3 tablespoons soy
sauce
2 teaspoons cornstrach
2 tablespoons cold water
1 tablespoon pimiento,
chopped
1 9½-ounce can chow
mein noodles, heated
or cooked rice

1 . Moisten chicken pieces with water. Sprinkle liberally with
MICRO SHAKE to coat all surfaces.

2 . In a 2-quart shallow baking dish, arrange chicken. Microwave,
covered, on HIGH for 7 minutes.

3 . Add celery. Microwave, covered, on HIGH for 1 minute. Add
canned vegetables and water chestnuts.

4 . In a small bowl, combine soy sauce, cornstarch and water.
Pour over chicken and vegetables. Stir to combine with pan
juices.

5 . Microwave, covered, on HIGH for 5 minutes or until thickened. Stir once during cooking. Add pimiento.

6 . Let stand, covered, 5 minutes before serving over chow mein
noodles or rice.

Serves 4 to 6.

Oriental Chicken with Rice

1 8-ounce can water
   chestnuts, sliced
1 ⅓ cup water
1 6½-ounce box
   packaged pre-cooked
   long grain and wild
   rice
1 4-ounce can
   mushrooms, sliced

2 whole chicken breasts,
   halved, boned and skin
   removed
MICRO SHAKE - Chicken
   Flavor
2 tablespoons soy sauce
1 10¾-ounce can
   condensed golden
   cream of mushroom
   soup

1 . Drain liquid from water chestnuts and add to water in a
    2-quart oblong baking dish. Stir in rice and seasoning packets.
    Microwave, covered, on HIGH for 5 minutes. Stir.

2 . Layer water chestnuts and mushrooms over rice.

3 . Moisten chicken pieces with water. Sprinkle liberally with
    MICRO SHAKE to coat all surfaces.

4 . Lay chicken pieces on top of mushrooms.

5 . In a small bowl, combine soy sauce and soup. Mix well.
    Spoon over chicken pieces.

6 . Microwave, covered, on HIGH for 25 to 28 minutes.

7 . Let stand, covered, 5 minutes.

Serves 4.

NOTES _____

_____

_____

_____

_____

_____

_____

Mexican Chicken Kiev

4 whole chicken breasts, halved, boned and skin removed
¼ teaspoon chili powder
½ teaspoon cumin
MICRO SHAKE - Chicken Flavor

¼ pound Monterey Jack cheese
1 4-ounce can diced green chiles
2 tablespoons butter or margarine

1 . Pound chicken breasts with flat side of meat mallet to ¼-inch thickness.

2 . In a small bowl, combine chili powder, cumin and 4 teaspoons MICRO SHAKE. Sprinkle inside surface of flattened breasts with ¼ teaspoon spice mixture.

3 . Cut Monterey Jack cheese in 8 pieces. Place a piece of cheese and 1 tablespoon green chiles on each chicken breast. Fold end over cheese. Fold in sides, then continue rolling. Secure seam with wooden pick.

4 . Moisten outer sides of each roll with water. Sprinkle to coat outer surfaces of chicken rolls with remaining spice mixture. In a 2-quart shallow casserole, place butter. Microwave on HIGH for 30 seconds. Place chicken rolls in casserole, seam side down.

5 . Microwave, covered with wax paper, on HIGH for 8 to 10 minutes. Drizzle pieces with remaining juices on bottom of dish.

6 . Let stand, covered, 5 minutes.

Serves 4 to 6.

Italian Lemon Chicken

2½ to 3 pounds chicken parts, skin removed
MICRO SHAKE - Chicken Flavor
4 tablespoons butter or margarine

Juice of 1 lemon
⅓ cup parsley
1 teaspoon garlic powder
½ teaspoon Italian seasoning

1 . Moisten chicken pieces with water. Sprinkle liberally with MICRO SHAKE to coat all surfaces.

2 . In a 2-quart shallow baking dish, place butter and 1 tablespoon MICRO SHAKE. Microwave on HIGH for 30 seconds. Add remaining ingredients. Stir well.

3 . Arrange chicken pieces over sauce, placing meatiest pieces towards outer edge of dish.

4 . Microwave, covered, on HIGH for 16 to 18 minutes or until done.

5 . Let stand, covered, 5 minutes.

Serves 4.

Wined Cornish Game Hens

1½ teaspoons rosemary leaves
½ cup dry white wine

2 Cornish Game Hens, halved
MICRO SHAKE - Chicken Flavor

1 . In a small bowl, soak rosemary leaves in wine.

2 . In a 2-quart oblong baking dish, arrange hens cut side down. Moisten with white wine. Sprinkle liberally with MICRO SHAKE to coat all surfaces.

3 . Pour wine mixture around (not over) hens.

4 . Microwave, covered, on HIGH for 10 minutes.

5 . Rearrange hens moving center halves to outer side of dish.

6 . Microwave, covered, on HIGH for 8 to 10 minutes.

7 . Let stand, covered, 5 minutes.

Serves 2 to 4.

Brandied Cranberry Hens

1 cup orange marmalade
1 tablespoon cornstarch
1 16-ounce can whole
  cranberry sauce
2 tablespoons brandy
2 Cornish Game Hens,
  giblets removed

1 small orange, peeled,
  cut into eighths
1 small onion, quartered
MICRO SHAKE - Chicken
  Flavor

1 . In a medium mixing bowl, combine orange marmalade and
     cornstarch. Mix well. Add cranberry sauce. Microwave on
     HIGH for 5 to 6 minutes or until mixture boils and becomes
     clear. Add brandy, stirring well. Microwave on HIGH for 1 to
     2 minutes. Set aside.

2 . Sprinkle cavity of each hen with MICRO SHAKE. Stuff cavity
     of each hen with 2 onion quarters and 2 orange eighths.

3 . Moisten each hen with water. Sprinkle liberally with MICRO
     SHAKE to coat all surfaces.

4 . In a 2-quart oblong baking dish, place hens breast side up.
     Microwave, covered, on HIGH for 14 to 16 minutes. Rear-
     range hens so sides which were near outer edge of dish are in
     the center. Baste with 1 cup cranberry sauce.

5 . Microwave, covered, on HIGH for 2 to 4 minutes or until
     juices run clear.

6 . Let stand, covered, 5 minutes before serving with remaining
     sauce.

Serves 2 to 4.

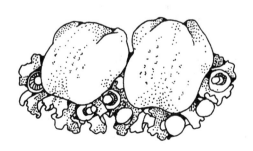

Peachy-Brandy Cornish Game Hens

6 tablespoons butter or
margarine
1 6½-ounce box pack-
aged pre-cooked long
grain and wild rice
1 2½-ounce package
sliced almonds
½ cup onion, chopped
10 medium mushrooms,
sliced

½ cup raisins
1 16-ounce can peach
halves
1 teaspoon poultry
seasoning
3 tablespoons brandy
4 Cornish Game Hens
MICRO SHAKE - Chicken
Flavor

1. In a large mixing bowl, combine 2 cups water, 2 tablespoons butter and rice seasoning packet. Microwave on HIGH for 6 minutes.

2. Add rice to mixture, cover with plastic wrap and let stand for 10 minutes.

3. In a medium bowl, combine almonds, onions, mushrooms and 4 tablespoons butter. Microwave, covered tightly, on HIGH for 4 minutes. Add raisins and continue microwaving on HIGH for 2 minutes. Dice 2 peaches and add to mixture.

4. Mix onion mixture with cooked rice. Add poultry seasoning, brandy and ¼ cup peach juice to mixture. Stir well.

5. Remove giblets from hens. Sprinkle cavity of each hen with MICRO SHAKE. Stuff with rice mixture.

6. Moisten each hen with water. Sprinkle liberally with MICRO SHAKE to coat all surfaces.

7. In a shallow casserole, place hens breast side up. Microwave, covered with wax paper, on HIGH for 18 minutes. Rearrange hens so sides which were near outer edge of dish are in the center. Baste with drippings.

8. Microwave, covered, on HIGH for 5 minutes or until legs move easily and juices run clear.

9. Let stand, covered, 5 minutes.

10. Microwave remaining rice mixture, covered, on HIGH for 4 minutes. Serve hens with sauce and peach halves.

Serves 4 to 6.

Cornish Game Hens
with Curry Dressing

1 tablespoon butter
2 tablespoons celery, minced
1 tablespoon onion, minced
1½ teaspoon curry powder
1 cup apple juice
⅓ cup packaged pre-cooked rice
½ cup chopped mushrooms
½ crisp apple, peeled and chopped
2 tablespoons walnuts, chopped
2 tablespoons raisins
2 Cornish Game Hens
MICRO SHAKE - Chicken Flavor

1 . In a 2-quart casserole, place butter. Microwave on HIGH for 30 seconds or until melted. Add celery, onion and curry. Stir.

2 . Microwave on HIGH for 1 minute or until vegetables are tender. Add apple juice and rice.

3 . Microwave, covered with plastic wrap, on HIGH for 10 minutes. Add mushrooms, apples, walnuts, and raisins.

4 . Remove giblets from hens. Sprinkle cavity of each hen with MICRO SHAKE. Stuff.

5 . Moisten each hen with water. Sprinkle liberally with MICRO SHAKE to coat all surfaces.

6 . In a 2-quart shallow baking dish, place hens breast side up. Microwave, covered, on HIGH for 16 to 20 minutes or until juices run clear.

7 . Let stand, covered, 5 minutes.

Serves 2 to 4.

Roast Turkey

8 to 12 pound turkey
Favorite stuffing
MICRO SHAKE - Chicken Flavor

1 . Sprinkle cavity of turkey with MICRO SHAKE. Stuff. Secure openings with wooden picks and tie legs. Moisten turkey with water, apple juice or white wine. Sprinkle liberally with MICRO SHAKE to coat all sides.

2 . Place turkey breast side down in a baking dish. Microwave, covered with wax paper, on HIGH for 10 minutes. While microwaving, calculate total cooking time by allowing 12 to 15 minutes per pound. Divide time into half. After first 10 minutes of cooking, reduce power to MEDIUM and microwave first half of cooking time.

3 . Check turkey occasionally and shield areas that might be over-cooking with small pieces of foil. Baste with drippings.

4 . Turn turkey breast side up and microwave for second half of calculated cooking time or until turkey is done.

5 . Turkey is done when leg moves freely when pressed and internal temperature at meatiest part of thigh registers 175° Farhenheit with a meat thermometer. Also juices run clear when breast meat under wing is pierced with a fork.

6 . Let stand, tented with foil, 20 minutes before carving.

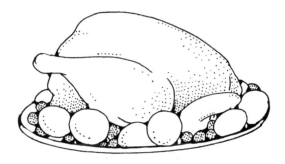

Cranberry Sauce

1 pound fresh
  cranberries
1½ cups sugar

¼ cup water
½ cup orange
  marmalade

1 . In a large mixing bowl, place cranberries, sugar and water. Microwave on HIGH for 6 minutes. Stir well.

2 . Add orange marmalade. Microwave on HIGH for 2 minutes.

3 . Pour into mold or serving bowl. Refrigerate before serving.

Serves 6 to 8.

Golden Brown Turkey Breast

3 to 4 pound turkey breast
MICRO SHAKE - Chicken Flavor

1 . Moisten all sides of turkey breast with water. Sprinkle liberally with MICRO SHAKE to coat all sides.

2 . In a 2-quart baking dish, place turkey breast side down. Calculate total cooking time by using 8 minutes per pound. Microwave, covered with wax paper, on HIGH for one-half the total cooking time.

3 . Turn breast side up. Sprinkle with MICRO SHAKE. Baste with drippings.

4 . Microwave, covered, for second half of calculated cooking time or until internal temperature of meatiest area is 170° Fahrenheit with a meat thermometer. Baste with drippings.

5 . Let stand, tented with foil, 5 to 10 minutes before carving.

Serves 6 to 8.

Golden Goose

8 to 10 pound domestic
goose
MICRO SHAKE - Chicken
Flavor

1 slice onion
2 stalks celery
Red wine or water

1 . Sprinkle cavity of goose with MICRO SHAKE. Place onion and celery in cavity. Secure openings with wooden picks and tie legs. Moisten goose with water or wine. Sprinkle liberally with MICRO SHAKE to coat all sides.

2 . Place goose breast side down in a baking dish. Microwave, covered with wax paper, on HIGH for 10 minutes. While microwaving, calculate total cooking time by allowing 12 to 15 minutes per pound. Divide time into half. After first 10 minutes of cooking, reduce power to MEDIUM and microwave first half of cooking time.

3 . After first half of cooking drain off fat. Baste with drippings.

4 . Turn goose breast side up and microwave for second half of calculated cooking time or until goose is done.

5 . Goose is done when juices run clear when breast meat under wing is pierced with a fork.

6 . Let stand, tented with foil, 15 minutes before carving.

Serves 7 to 8.

NOTES

International

HOUSE SPECIAL

Bev's Eggplant Parmesan with Meat

1 large eggplant, sliced
   ¼-inch thick
MICRO SHAKE - Meat
   Flavor
¼ cup olive oil
1 pound lean ground
   beef

1 cup onion, chopped
1 15½-ounce jar plain
   spaghetti sauce
2 tablespoons Parmesan
   cheese, grated

1 .   In a 2-quart shallow baking dish, layer eggplant. Sprinkle each layer liberally with MICRO SHAKE to cover all surfaces. Drizzle each layer with olive oil.

2 .   Microwave, covered, on HIGH For 7 minutes or until tender. Set aside, covered.

3 .   In a colander with drip pan, crumble ground beef. Add onion. Sprinkle with 1 tablespoon MICRO SHAKE. Microwave on HIGH for 5 minutes. Stir to break up.

4 .   In a large mixing bowl, combine meat mixture with spaghetti sauce. Microwave, covered, on HIGH for 7 minutes.

5 .   Remove eggplant from dish. Drain water. Place a layer of eggplant on bottom of dish. Spread meat sauce alternating with layers of eggplant.

6 .   Sprinkle with Parmesan cheese. Microwave, covered, on HIGH for 10 minutes.

7 .   Let stand, covered, 5 minutes.

Serves 4 to 6.

Chicken Italiano

1 cup Italian salad dressing
MICRO SHAKE - Chicken Flavor
2½ to 3 pounds chicken parts

1 . In a 2-quart shallow baking dish, combine salad dressing and 1 tablespoon MICRO SHAKE. Stir well.

2 . Place chicken pieces in marinade. Cover and refrigerate for at least 1 hour.

3 . Drain marinade from baking dish.

4 . Rearrange chicken pieces in baking dish with meatiest pieces towards outer edge of dish. Sprinkle each piece liberally with MICRO SHAKE to coat all surfaces.

5 . Microwave, covered with wax paper, on HIGH for 18 to 20 minutes.

6 . Let stand, covered, 5 minutes.

Serves 4.

Hamburger Italiano

1 pound lean ground beef
¼ teaspoon oregano leaves
2 tablespoons Parmesan cheese, grated

2 tablespoons catsup
MICRO SHAKE - Meat Flavor

1 . In a medium mixing bowl, combine all ingredients except MICRO SHAKE. Blend well.

2 . Shape ground beef into four patties. Moisten both sides of each patty with water. Sprinkle each side liberally with MICRO SHAKE.

3 . In a 2-quart dish or baking rack, place patties. Microwave, covered with wax paper, on HIGH for 7 to 9 minutes.

4 . Let stand, covered, 3 minutes.

Serves 4.

Chicken Caccitore

2½ to 3 pounds chicken parts
MICRO SHAKE - Chicken Flavor
1 cup onion, chopped
1 cup green pepper, chopped
1 clove garlic, crushed

2 tablespoons butter or margarine
1 teaspoon Italian seasoning
1 16-ounce can whole, peeled tomatoes, undrained
6 fresh mushrooms, sliced

1 . Moisten chicken pieces with water. Sprinkle each piece liberally with MICRO SHAKE to coat all surfaces.

2 . In a 2-quart shallow baking dish, arrange chicken pieces with meatiest pieces towards outer edge of dish. Microwave, covered with wax paper, on HIGH for 10 minutes. Set aside.

3 . In a medium mixing bowl, place onion, green pepper, garlic, butter and Italian seasoning. Microwave, covered with plastic wrap, on HIGH for 4 minutes or until vegetables are tender.

4 . Add tomatoes and mushrooms to vegetable mixture. Stir well.

5 . Pour vegetable mixture around cooked chicken pieces. Microwave, covered with wax paper, on HIGH for 12 to 15 minutes or until done.

6 . Let stand, covered, 5 minutes.

Serves 4 to 6.

Beef Cordon Bleu

1 pound beef sirloin
steak, ¼-inch thick
4 thin slices proscuitto
or ham
¼ pound Monterey Jack
cheese, cut in 3-inch
sticks

MICRO SHAKE - Meat
Flavor
2 tablespoons butter or
margarine
2 tablespoons dry white
wine
Snipped parsley

1 . Trim fat from steak and cut into 4 pieces. Flatten beef with mallet to ¹/₈-inch thickness.

2 . Roll proscuitto around cheese sticks and place each bundle on a piece of beef.

3 . Fold beef over and secure with wooden picks. Moisten surfaces of beef pieces with water. Sprinkle to coat outer sides of each meat roll with MICRO SHAKE.

4 . In a 2-quart shallow baking dish, place butter. Microwave on HIGH for 30 seconds. Place beef rolls in melted butter. Microwave, covered with wax paper, on HIGH for 6 minutes or until desired degree of doneness.

5 . Transfer beef to serving platter and remove picks. Add wine to butter in dish. Swirl around and drizzle over beef. Garnish with parsley.

Serves 4.

Salisbury Steaks

MICRO SHAKE - Meat
  Flavor
1 tablespoon flour
¼ cup water

¼ cup onion, chopped
½ cup mushrooms,
  sliced
1 pound lean ground
  beef

1 . In a small bowl, mix ½ teaspoon MICRO SHAKE, flour and water. Set aside.

2 . In a 2-quart shallow baking dish, place onions and water mixture. Microwave, covered with plastic wrap, for 1 minute.

3 . Add sliced mushrooms. Microwave, covered with plastic wrap, on HIGH for 1 minute. Stir well.

4 . Shape ground beef into 4 hamburger steaks.

5 . Moisten both sides of each steak with water. Sprinkle each side liberally with MICRO SHAKE.

6 . Arrange steaks on gravy mixture.

7 . Microwave, covered with plastic wrap, on HIGH for 7 to 9 minutes or until desired degree of doneness.

8 . Let stand, covered, 3 minutes. Spoon gravy over steaks and serve.

Serves 4.

Beef Stroganoff

1½ pounds boneless lean
   round steak
MICRO SHAKE - Meat
   Flavor
½ cup onion, chopped
1 cup hot tap water
¼ cup sherry

2 tablespoons cornstarch
1 8-ounce can mushroom
   stems and pieces,
   drained
1 cup sour cream
1 tablespoon parsley
   flakes

1 . Cut meat diagonally into thin bite-sized pieces. In a 2-quart casserole, place meat pieces. Sprinkle liberally with MICRO SHAKE. Pierce meat with a fork.

2 . Microwave, covered with wax paper, on HIGH for 6 minutes or until no longer pink. Stir well. Set aside.

3 . In a small bowl, place onion, 2 tablespoons water and ½ teaspoon MICRO SHAKE. Microwave, covered with plastic wrap, on HIGH for 2 minutes.

4 . In a medium bowl, combine hot water, sherry and cornstarch. Pour liquid over meat mixture. Add mushrooms. Microwave, covered with wax paper, on HIGH for 13 to 15 minutes, stirring twice.

5 . Beat sour cream until smooth; slowly blend into meat mixture. Garnish with parsley and serve over hot cooked rice or noodles.

Serves 4.

Chicken Kiev

½ teaspoon snipped
  chives
Dash white pepper
Dash garlic powder
2 tablespoons butter
  (hard)

2 whole chicken breasts,
  halved, boned and skin
  removed
MICRO SHAKE - Chicken
  Flavor

1 . In a small bowl, combine chives, pepper and garlic powder.

2 . Pound chicken with flat side of meat mallet to ¼-inch thickness. Moisten inside surface of flattened breasts with water. Sprinkle MICRO SHAKE on inside of each piece.

3 . Cut butter into 4 equal pieces. Roll in chive mixture.

4 . Place butter at one end of pounded chicken breast. Fold end over butter. Fold in sides, then continue rolling. Secure seam with wooden pick.

5 . Moisten outer sides of each roll with water. Sprinkle to coat outer surfaces of chicken breasts with MICRO SHAKE. In a 2-quart shallow baking dish, place chicken breasts, seam side down.

6 . Microwave, covered with wax paper, on HIGH for 5 minutes. Drizzle pieces with juices in bottom of dish.

7 . Let stand, covered, 3 minutes.

Serves 2 to 4.

Teriyaki Chicken

2 whole chicken breasts, halved, boned and skin removed
MICRO SHAKE - Chicken Flavor
2 tablespoons catsup
1 tablespoon vinegar
¼ cup oil
¼ cup soy sauce
⅛ teaspoon garlic powder
1 green pepper, cut into rings

1 .   Moisten chicken with water. Sprinkle each piece liberally with MICRO SHAKE to coat all surfaces.

2 .   In a 1½-quart shallow baking dish, combine catsup, vinegar, oil, soy sauce and garlic powder. Mix well.

3 .   Place chicken breasts on sauce. Top with rings of bell pepper.

4 .   Microwave, covered, on HIGH for 5 to 7 minutes or until done. Let stand, covered, for 4 minutes.

Serves 4.

Easy Moussaka

2 tablespoons olive or vegetable oil
1 small eggplant, sliced ¼-inch thick
½ onion, thinly sliced
6 mushrooms, sliced
½ green pepper, cut into strips
1 tomato, sliced
2 cloves garlic, finely diced
¾ teaspoon coriander, optional
¾ teaspoon allspice, optional
¼ teaspoon pepper
1 tablespoon lemon juice
MICRO SHAKE - Meat Flavor
1 pound ground lamb or beef
Parsley, finely chopped

1 .   In a 2-quart shallow baking dish, spread 1 tablespoon olive oil. Layer vegetables in casserole in order given. Sprinkle 1 tablespoon olive oil, spices and lemon juice. Sprinkle MICRO SHAKE over entire dish.

2 .   Microwave, covered, on HIGH for 8 minutes.

3 .   Crumble ground lamb or beef over vegetables. Top with parsley. Shake MICRO SHAKE liberally over meat.

4 .   Microwave, covered, on HIGH for 7 to 9 minutes.

5 .   Let stand, covered, 2 to 4 minutes. Serve with rice.

Serves 4.

Baghdad Lamb Shanks with Rice

1 cup tomato juice
½ cup onion, chopped
1 small clove garlic,
   minced
MICRO SHAKE - Meat
   Flavor
½ teaspoon allspice,
   optional
½ teaspoon coriander,
   optional

4 lamb shanks (approxi-
   mately 3 pounds)
⅔ cup long grain white
   rice, uncooked
1 cup tomatoes, chopped
1 tablespoon parsley
   flakes

1 . In a 3-quart deep casserole, combine tomato juice, onion, garlic, 4 teaspoons MICRO SHAKE, allspice and coriander.

2 . Moisten lamb shanks with water. Pierce meat with a fork. Sprinkle each shank liberally with MICRO SHAKE to coat all surfaces. Place meat in tomato juice mixture.

3 . Microwave, covered, on HIGH for 6 minutes. Reduce to MEDIUM and continue to microwave for 20 minutes.

4 . Lift shanks out; add uncooked rice, chopped tomatoes and parsley flakes. Mix well. Place lamb shanks on top of rice mixture.

5 . Microwave, covered, on MEDIUM for 20 minutes. Turn lamb shanks over and skim off fat.

6 . Microwave, covered, on MEDIUM for 10 to 15 minutes or until rice is tender.

7 . Let stand, covered, 5 minutes.

Serves 4.

Greek Lamb Kabob

1 cup dry white wine
2 tablespoons olive oil
1 tablespoon lemon juice
1 large clove garlic,
   minced
MICRO SHAKE - Meat
   Flavor
1 pound lamb, cut into
   1-inch cubes

1 medium green pepper,
   cut into 1-inch cubes
1 medium onion, cut
   into 1-inch cubes
6 medium mushrooms,
   quartered
8 cherry tomatoes, sliced

1 . Moisten meat with water. Sprinkle liberally with MICRO
SHAKE. Pierce meat with a fork. Set aside.

2 . In a 2-quart shallow baking dish, combine wine, olive oil,
lemon juice, garlic and 1 tablespoon MICRO SHAKE. Stir well.

3 . Add lamb and vegetables to the marinade. Cover and
refrigerate for at least 1 hour. Stir occasionally.

4 . On a 12-inch round platter, arrange lamb cubes in a circle
around outer edge of platter. Place green pepper cubes next to
meat, then onions and mushrooms. End with tomatoes piled
in center of platter.

5 . Sprinkle MICRO SHAKE liberally over meat and vegetables.

6 . Microwave, covered with wax paper, on HIGH for 13 to 15
minutes or until meat is desired degree of doneness.

7 . Let stand, covered, 5 minutes before serving over a bed of rice
or as appetizers.

Serves 4.

Vegetables

Country "Fried" Potatoes

1 cup onion, chopped
2 tablespoons vegetable
  oil
3 tablespoons MICRO
  SHAKE - Chicken
  Flavor

2 large potatoes (about
  1 pound), peeled and
  thinly sliced

1 . In a 2-quart casserole, place onion and 1 tablespoon
    vegetable oil. Sprinkle with 1 tablespoon MICRO SHAKE
    to coat onions. Microwave, covered, on HIGH for 3
    minutes.

2 . Add potatoes to onions. Stir well with an additional
    tablespoon of oil. Add 2 tablespoons MICRO SHAKE.
    Mix well. Microwave, covered, on HIGH for 6 minutes.
    Stir well.

3 . Microwave, covered, on HIGH for 4 to 6 minutes or until
    tender.

4 . Let stand, covered, 2 minutes.

Serves 4.

Micro-Brown Potatoes

2 tablespoons butter or
  margarine
6 small red potatoes,
  peeled, cut into
  quarters

½ medium onion, cut
  into wedges
1 teaspoon MICRO
  SHAKE - Meat Flavor

1 . In a small casserole, place butter. Microwave on HIGH for 30
     seconds. Place potatoes on melted butter. Arrange onions
     around potatoes. Sprinkle with MICRO SHAKE.

2 . Microwave, covered, on HIGH for 9 to 11 minutes or until
     tender.

3 . Let stand, covered, 2 minutes.

Serves 4.

Plantation Potatoes

1 cup corn flakes,
  crushed
5 tablespoons butter or
  margarine
2 large potatoes (about
  1 pound)
2 tablespoons minced
  onion

3 tablespoons parsley
  flakes
¼ teaspoon garlic
  powder
1½ tablespoons MICRO
  SHAKE - Meat Flavor

1 . In a small bowl, place corn flakes and 1 tablespoon butter.
     Microwave on HIGH for 1 minute. Stir well.

2 . Scrub and thinly slice potatoes.

3 . In a 2-quart casserole, combine potatoes, onion, garlic, parsley
     and MICRO SHAKE. Mix well. Cut remaining butter into
     pieces and distribute over potatoes.

4 . Microwave, covered, on HIGH for 8 minutes.

5 . Stir the corn flake mixture into potatoes. Microwave, un-
     covered, on HIGH for 2 to 4 minutes.

6 . Let stand 2 minutes.

Serves 4.

Creamed Hash Browns

½ cup onion, chopped
6 tablespoons butter or
  margarine
2 teaspoons MICRO
  SHAKE - Chicken
  Flavor
1 2-pound bag frozen
  hash brown potatoes

1 10¾-ounce can
  condensed cream of
  chicken soup
2 cups Cheddar cheese,
  shredded
1 cup sour cream
1½ cups corn flakes,
  crushed

1. In a 3-quart deep casserole, place frozen potatoes. Microwave on HIGH for 10 minutes.

2. In a small bowl, place onion, 2 tablespoons butter and 1 teaspoon MICRO SHAKE. Microwave, covered, on HIGH for 2 minutes.

3. Add onion, soup, cheese, sour cream and 1 teaspoon MICRO SHAKE to potatoes. Stir well.

4. In a small bowl, place 4 tablespoons butter. Microwave on HIGH for 30 seconds. Add corn flakes. Stir well. Sprinkle on top of potatoes to cover all.

5. Microwave on HIGH for 15 minutes.

6. Let stand 2 minutes.

Serves 8.

NOTES _____

_____

_____

_____

_____

_____

_____

Potato Salad

4 to 5 potatoes (about
  1½ pounds), peeled
  and thinly sliced
3 eggs
¼ cup onion, chopped
½ cup celery, chopped
¾ cup salad dressing
2 teaspoons prepared
  mustard

2 teaspoons vinegar
1 teaspoon sugar
½ teaspoon salt
½ teaspoon garlic
  powder
Paprika
Parsley

1 . In a 3-quart deep casserole, place potatoes. Microwave, covered, on HIGH for 9 to 11 minutes. Allow to cool.

2 . Crack eggs into custard cups. Microwave, covered, on MEDIUM HIGH for 2 to 3 minutes or until yolk is hard. Chop into pieces.

3 . Add cooked eggs, onion and celery to potatoes.

4 . In a small bowl, combine salad dressing, mustard, vinegar, sugar, salt and garlic powder. Stir well.

5 . Pour over potato mixture and toss gently to mix well. Sprinkle with paprika. Garnish with parsley.

Serves 6.

Rice A La Micro Shake

1½ cups water
2½ teaspoons MICRO
   SHAKE - Meat or
   Chicken Flavor

2 teaspoons butter
1½ cups packaged pre-
   cooked rice

1 . In a 1-quart bowl, combine water, MICRO SHAKE and butter.

2 . Microwave on HIGH for 5 minutes or until it reaches a full boil.

3 . Stir in rice. Microwave on HIGH for 15 to 20 seconds.

4 . Let stand, covered, 5 minutes. Fluff with fork.

Serves 4.

Vegetable Rice

⅓ cup carrots, chopped
⅓ cup celery, chopped
¼ cup onion, chopped
2 tablespoons butter or
   margarine

1½ cups water
5½ teaspoons MICRO
   SHAKE - Chicken
   Flavor
1½ cups packaged pre-
   cooked rice

1 . In a small bowl combine carrot, celery, onion, 1 tablespoon butter and 1 tablespoon MICRO SHAKE.

2 . Microwave, covered, on HIGH for 3 minutes. Set aside.

3 . In a 2-quart bowl, combine water, 2½ teaspoons MICRO SHAKE and 2 teaspoons butter.

4 . Microwave on HIGH for 5 minutes or until it reaches a full boil.

5 . Stir in rice. Microwave on HIGH for 15 to 20 seconds.

6 . Let stand, covered, 5 minutes. Fluff with fork. Add vegetable mixture to rice.

Serves 4.

Christmas Rice

2 tablespoons green pepper, diced
3 tablespoons onion, diced
2½ tablespoons MICRO SHAKE - Chicken Flavor
1½ cups water

2 teaspoons butter or margarine
2 teaspoons parsley, chopped
1½ cups packaged pre-cooked rice
1 tablespoon pimiento, diced

1. In a small bowl, combine green pepper, onion, 1 tablespoon water and ½ teaspoon MICRO SHAKE.

2. Microwave, covered, on HIGH for 1 minute. Set aside.

3. In a 1-quart casserole, combine water, remaining MICRO SHAKE, butter and parsley.

4. Microwave on HIGH for 5 minutes or until it reaches a full boil.

5. Stir in rice. Microwave on HIGH for 15 to 20 seconds.

6. Let stand, covered, 5 minutes. Fluff with fork. Add pre-cooked vegetables and pimiento to rice.

Serves 4.

Spinach and Rice Casserole

1 cup onion, chopped
2 tablespoons butter or
    margarine
1½ cups water
1½ cups packaged pre-
    cooked rice
1 10-ounce package
    frozen chopped
    spinach

8 ounces processed
    cheese spread
1 10¾-ounce can
    condensed cream of
    mushroom soup
¼ teaspoon ground
    nutmeg

1. In a 1-quart bowl, place water. Microwave on HIGH for 5 minutes or until it reaches a full boil.

2. Stir in rice. Microwave on HIGH for 15 to 20 seconds.

3. In a small bowl, place onion and butter. Microwave, covered, on HIGH for 3 minutes.

4. Puncture frozen carton of spinach 4 times with a fork. Place box on a plate. Microwave on HIGH for 5 minutes. Drain well.

5. In a 2-quart casserole, combine onion, rice, spinach, cheese, soup and nutmeg.

6. Microwave on HIGH for 10 to 12 minutes. Stir well.

7. Let stand, covered, 5 minutes.

Serves 4 to 6.

Grandma's Creamed Spinach Casserole

2 15-ounce cans spinach
¾ cup milk
2 tablespoons butter or margarine
5 saltine crackers, crumbled

1 tablespoon fresh lemon juice
1 tablespoon Parmesan cheese, grated

1 .   Drain spinach well. Place in a 2-quart serving bowl. Add remaining ingredients, except Parmesan cheese. Stir well.

2 .   Microwave, covered, on HIGH for 4 minutes. Stir well.

3 .   Microwave, covered, on HIGH an additional 4 minutes. Stir well.

4 .   Let stand, covered, 5 minutes. Sprinkle with Parmesan cheese before serving.

Serves 4.

Broccoli & Cheese Casserole

1 10-ounce package
   frozen chopped
   broccoli
1 cup celery, chopped
1 cup mushroom, sliced
½ cup onion, chopped
2 tablespoons water
1 tablespoon MICRO
   SHAKE - Chicken
   Flavor

1 10¾-ounce can
   condensed cream of
   mushroom soup
8 ounces processed
   cheese spread,
   cut into pieces

1. Puncture frozen carton of broccoli 4 times with a fork. Place box on a plate. Microwave on HIGH for 5 minutes. Drain well.

2. In a 2-quart serving bowl, place celery, mushroom, onion, water, and MICRO SHAKE. Microwave, covered tightly, on HIGH for 5 minutes.

3. Add broccoli, soup and cheese to cooked vegetables.

4. Microwave, covered, on HIGH for 5 minutes. Stir well.

5. Let stand, covered, 5 minutes.

Serves 4.

NOTES _____

_____

_____

_____

_____

_____

Mushrooms Parmesan

1 pound fresh mushroom
caps
4 tablespoons butter or
margarine
¼ teaspoon garlic
powder

1 tablespoon MICRO
SHAKE - Chicken
Flavor
¼ teaspoon oregano
leaves
1 tablespoon Parmesan
cheese, grated

1 . Wash mushrooms, remove the stems.

2 . In a shallow dish, place butter, garlic powder, MICRO SHAKE
and oregano. Microwave on HIGH for 1 minute or until
melted. Stir well.

3 . Dip each mushroom in butter mixture, coat well.

4 . In a 1-quart shallow baking dish, place mushrooms up in a
single layer. Microwave on HIGH for 5 minutes.

5 . Sprinkle with Parmesan cheese. Let stand for 5 minutes.

May serve as a vegetable with dinner or as an appetizer.

Serves 4 to 6.

Gardener's Special Platter

1 ½ pounds fresh
   broccoli
½ head cauliflower
2 medium zucchini,
   sliced
2 medium tomatoes, cut
   into wedges

3 tablespoons butter or
   margarine
2 teaspoons MICRO
   SHAKE - Chicken
   flavor
½ teaspoon garlic salt
½ cup Parmesan cheese,
   grated

1 . Trim broccoli; cut into pieces about 2 ½ inches long with stalks about ¼-inch thick. On a 12-inch round serving platter, arrange broccoli with flower ends toward outer edge.

2 . Cut cauliflower into similiar-sized floweretes. Place a row around platter next to broccoli.

3 . Place zucchini next to cauliflower.

4 . Mound the tomatoes in center of platter.

5 . Microwave, covered, on HIGH for 12 minutes.

6 . Let stand, covered, for 5 minutes.

7 . In a small bowl, place butter and MICRO SHAKE. Microwave on HIGH for 1 minute.

8 . Drizzle butter over vegetables. Sprinkle with garlic salt and Parmesan cheese.

Serve with a meal or as an appetizer with toothpicks.

Serves 4 to 6.

Zucchini & Tomatoes

2 tomatoes, cut into
  1-inch cubes
½ cup water
½ teaspoon salt
½ cup onion, chopped

1 zucchini, cut into
  ¼-inch slices
1 teaspoon basil leaves
1 teaspoon sugar

1 . In a 2-quart serving bowl, combine tomato, water and salt. Microwave, covered, on HIGH for 10 minutes.

2 . In a small bowl, place onion and 1 tablespoon water. Microwave, covered, on HIGH for 2 minutes.

3 . In a small bowl, place zucchini. Microwave, covered, on HIGH for 2 minutes.

4 . Add onion, zucchini, basil and sugar to tomatoes. Microwave, covered, on HIGH for 2 minutes.

5 . Let stand, covered, 3 minutes.

Serves 4.

Baked Carrots

6 medium carrots
4 tablespoons butter or
  margarine
1 tablespoon lemon juice
2 tablespoons brown
  sugar

1 teaspoon MICRO
  SHAKE - Chicken
  Flavor
1 tablespoon parsley,
  chopped

1 . Peel carrots and cut into 3-inch narrow strips.

2 . In a 2-quart serving bowl, place carrots.

3 . In a small bowl, combine butter, lemon juice, brown sugar and MICRO SHAKE. Microwave on HIGH for 1 minute.

4 . Drizzle melted butter mixture over carrots.

5 . Microwave, covered, on HIGH for 10 to 15 minutes or until carrots are tender.

6 . Let stand, covered, 5 minutes.

Serves 4.

Vegetables With Wine Sauce

1 green pepper, diced
½ pound fresh
  mushrooms, sliced
½ cup onion, chopped
4 tablespoons fresh
  parsley, snipped

2 tablespoons MICRO
  SHAKE - Chicken
  Flavor
½ cup sherry

1 .   In a 2-quart serving bowl, combine all ingredients. Stir well.

2 .   Microwave, covered with plastic wrap, on HIGH for 8 minutes. Stir well.

3 .   Let stand, covered, 3 minutes.

Serves 4.

Ratatouille

1 medium eggplant, cut
  into ½-inch cubes
1 medium green pepper,
  cut into strips
½ cup onion, chopped
2 cloves garlic, minced
¼ cup olive or vegetable
  oil
2 medium zucchini,
  cut into ¼-inch
  slices

2 teaspoons dried parsley
  flakes
1 teaspoon basil leaves
1 teaspoon oregano
  leaves
1 teaspoon MICRO
  SHAKE - Chicken
  Flavor
½ teaspoon sugar
3 medium tomatoes, cut
  into wedges

1 .   In a 3-quart deep casserole, combine all ingredients except tomatoes. Microwave, covered, on HIGH for 13 to 15 minutes or until vegetables are tender.

2 .   Gently mix in tomatoes. Microwave, covered, on HIGH for 2 minutes.

3 .   Let stand, covered, 3 minutes.

Serves 6.

Southern Baked Beans

3 slices bacon	2 tablespoons catsup
½ cup onion, chopped	1 teaspoon mustard
2 16-ounce cans pork	2 tablespoons molasses
and beans	Dash Worcestershire
¼ cup brown sugar	sauce

1 . In a 2-quart serving bowl, place bacon. Microwave, covered, on HIGH for 3 to 4 minutes or until crispy. Remove cooked bacon. Cut into ½-inch pieces and set aside.

2 . Place onion in bacon drippings. Microwave, covered, on HIGH for 2 minutes.

3 . Add pork and beans, bacon and remaining ingredients to onion. Stir well.

4 . Microwave, covered, on HIGH for 12 minutes.

5 . Let stand, covered, 3 minutes.

Serves 6.

Green Beans Almondine

½ cup almonds, sliced	1 teaspoon garlic
6 tablespoons butter or	powder
margarine	1 tablespoon MICRO
1 16-ounce package	SHAKE - Chicken
frozen French cut	Flavor
green beans	

1 . In a small bowl, place almonds and 2 tablespoons butter. Microwave on HIGH for 3 to 4 minutes, stirring after each minute.

2 . In a 2-quart serving bowl, place green beans. Microwave, covered with plastic wrap, on HIGH for 5 minutes. Let stand.

3 . In a small bowl, place 4 tablespoons butter, garlic powder and MICRO SHAKE. Microwave on HIGH for 30 seconds or until butter is melted.

4 . Drain any excess liquid from green beans. Toss with almonds. Drizzle with melted butter mixture. Stir well.

Serves 4 to 6.

Old Fashioned Green Beans

3 slices bacon, cut into 1-inch pieces
½ cup onion, chopped
2 1-pound cans cut green beans, drained

1 . In a 2-quart serving bowl, place bacon. Microwave, covered with paper towel, on HIGH for 3 to 4 minutes or until crisp.

2 . Remove cooked bacon. Set aside. Place onion in bacon drippings.

3 . Microwave, covered, on HIGH for 2 minutes.

4 . Add green beans and bacon to onion. Microwave, covered, on HIGH for 5 minutes.

5 . Let stand, covered, 2 minutes.

Serves 4 to 6.

Creole Green Beans

3 slices bacon, cut into 1-inch pieces
½ cup onion, chopped
1 teaspoon garlic powder
½ teaspoon Worcestershire sauce
Dash hot sauce
1 16-ounce can stewed tomatoes
1 16-ounce can cut green beans, drained
¼ cup almond slices

1 . In a 2-quart serving bowl, place bacon. Microwave, covered with paper towel, on HIGH for 3 to 4 minutes or until crisp. Remove bacon. Set aside.

2 . Place onion in bacon drippings. Microwave, covered, on HIGH for 2 minutes.

3 . Add garlic powder, Worcestershire sauce, hot sauce and stewed tomatoes. Stir well. Microwave, covered, on HIGH for 5 minutes.

4 . Add green beans and almonds. Mix lightly.

5 . Microwave, covered, on HIGH for 3 minutes or until hot.

6 . Let stand, covered, 3 minutes. Garnish with bacon.

Serves 4.

Scalloped Corn

1 16-ounce can creamed
  corn
1 16-ounce can whole
  kernal corn, drained
1 egg
4 tablespoons butter or
  margarine

1 teaspoon MICRO
  SHAKE - Chicken
  Flavor
¼ cup milk
10 saltine crackers,
  crumbled

1 . In a 2-quart serving bowl, combine all ingredients. Stir well.

2 . Microwave, covered, on HIGH for 10 minutes.

3 . Let stand, covered, 5 minutes.

Serves 6.

Peas and Pearl Onions

1 10-ounce package
  frozen peas
1 cup frozen whole small
  onions
4 tablespoons butter or
  margarine

1 tablespoon MICRO
  SHAKE - Chicken
  Flavor
1 teaspoon garlic powder
2 tablespoons Parmesan
  cheese, grated

1 . In a 2-quart serving bowl, combine peas and onions.
    Microwave, covered with plastic wrap, on HIGH for 7
    minutes.

2 . In a small bowl, place butter and MICRO SHAKE. Microwave
    on HIGH for 30 seconds.

3 . Drain any excess liquid from cooked vegetables. Stir well.
    Drizzle with melted butter. Sprinkle with garlic powder and
    cheese. Stir well.

Serves 4.

Asparagus With Hollandaise Sauce

1 bunch (¾ pound) fresh asparagus
¼ cup water

1 . Cut about ½-inch off ends of asparagus.

2 . In a 2-quart shallow baking dish, place asparagus with tips toward center. Add water. Microwave, covered with plastic wrap, on HIGH for 6 minutes or until tender.

3 . Let stand, covered, while preparing Hollandaise sauce.

Hollandaise Sauce

½ cup butter
1 tablespoon fresh lemon juice
3 egg yolks, beaten

1 . In a small bowl, place butter and lemon juice. Microwave on HIGH for 2 minutes or until bubbly.

2 . Slowly add melted butter to egg yolks, beating constantly with whisk or rotary beater. Serve immediately. Do not return to microwave oven to reheat.

Makes ¾ cup.

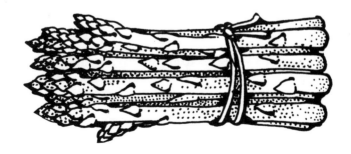

Eggplant Parmesan

1 1-pound eggplant,
  sliced ¼-inch thick
¼ cup olive oil
MICRO SHAKE - Meat
  Flavor
1 teaspoon garlic powder
1 teaspoon oregano
  leaves

1 15½-ounce jar plain
  spaghetti sauce
1 tablespoon Parmesan
  cheese, grated
1 tablespoon parsley
  flakes

1 .   In a 2-quart shallow baking dish, layer eggplant. Sprinkle each layer liberally with MICRO SHAKE to cover all surfaces. Drizzle each layer with olive oil. Sprinkle garlic powder and oregano over top layer of eggplant.

2 .   Microwave, covered, on HIGH for 7 minutes.

3 .   In a medium bowl, pour spaghetti sauce. Microwave, covered, on HIGH for 5 minutes.

4 .   Remove eggplant from dish. Drain water. Place a layer of eggplant on bottom of dish. Spread sauce alternating with layers of eggplant.

5 .   Microwave, covered, on HIGH for 5 minutes.

6 .   Sprinkle Parmesan cheese and parsley over top. Microwave, covered, on HIGH for 1 minute or until cheese is melted.

7 .   Let stand, covered, 5 minutes.

Serves 4 to 6.

Eggs, Quiches and Omelets

HOUSE SPECIAL

Mini Artichoke Quiche

2 6-ounce jars marin-
   ated artichoke hearts
½ cup onion, finely
   chopped
1 large clove garlic,
   finely minced
4 large eggs
¼ cup fine dry bread
   crumbs

¼ teaspoon salt
¼ teaspoon oregano
¼ teaspoon pepper
2 tablespoons parsley
   flakes
2 cups Cheddar cheese,
   shredded

1 . In a small bowl, drain marinade from 1 jar of artichoke
    hearts. Add onion and garlic. Microwave, covered, on
    HIGH for 2 minutes or until onion is transparent and
    tender.

2 . Drain marinade from other jar and refrigerate for use in
    salad dressing. Finely chop artichokes.

3 . In a medium mixing bowl, beat eggs. Stir in bread
    crumbs, seasonings, parsley, artichokes, cheese and
    onion mixture. Stir well.

4 . Pour mixture evenly into custard cups. Microwave 5
    cups at a time on MEDIUM HIGH for 5 minutes.

5 . Let stand 2 minutes.

Makes 10.

Egg Vegetable Pie

1 9-inch frozen pie crust	2 tablespoons butter
¼ cup onion, chopped	1 tablespoon MICRO
1 medium zucchini,	SHAKE - Chicken
shredded	Flavor
1 medium carrot,	1 cup Cheddar cheese,
shredded	shredded
1 cup mushroom, sliced	Basic Omelet Recipe on
	following page

1 . Transfer frozen pie crust into a 9-inch glass pie plate. Prick four times with a fork. Microwave on HIGH for 4 minutes.

2 . In a medium bowl, combine onion, zucchini, carrot, mushroom, butter and MICRO SHAKE. Microwave, covered tightly, on HIGH for 4 minutes.

3 . Prepare Basic Omelet recipe. Place cooked omelet in bottom of cooked pie crust. Spread vegetables over omelet. Top with cheese.

4 . Microwave on HIGH for 5 minutes or until cheese is melted.

5 . Let stand 2 minutes.

Serves 4 to 6.

Wisconsin Scramble

1 teaspoon MICRO
SHAKE - Chicken
Flavor
¼ cup milk or water
4 eggs

1 tablespoon butter or
margarine
¼ cup Cheddar cheese,
shredded

1 . In a small bowl, combine MICRO SHAKE with milk or water. Add eggs. Blend well.

2 . In a medium bowl, place butter. Microwave on HIGH for 30 seconds.

3 . Add egg mixture to butter. Microwave on HIGH for 2 minutes. Stir. Microwave an additional 30 seconds. Add cheese and stir well. Continue microwaving on HIGH for 30 to 60 seconds or until cheese is melted.

4 . Let stand, covered, for 2 minutes.

Serves 2.

Basic Omelet

4 eggs
4 tablespoons water or
milk
½ teaspoon salt

⅛ teaspoon pepper
1 tablespoon butter or
margarine

1 . In a medium bowl, combine eggs, water, salt and pepper. Beat eggs well.

2 . In a 9-inch pie plate, place butter. Microwave on HIGH for 30 seconds. Spread butter to cover plate.

3 . Pour egg mixture into pie plate. Microwave, covered with plastic wrap, on HIGH for 2 minutes.

4 . Tilt plate to move cooked eggs toward center. Microwave, covered, on HIGH for 1 to 2 minutes or until omelet is firm.

5 . Let stand, covered, 1 to 2 minutes.

Serves 2.

Mexican Omelet

4 eggs
4 tablespoons water or
  milk
½ teaspoon salt
⅛ teaspoon pepper
1 tablespoon butter or
  margarine

1 avocado, cut into
  1-inch pieces
½ cup sour cream
1 small tomato, cut into
  1-inch pieces
3 tablespoons salsa
½ cup Monterey Jack
  cheese, shredded

1 . In a medium bowl, combine eggs, water, salt and pepper. Beat eggs well.

2 . In a 9-inch pie plate, place butter. Microwave on HIGH for 30 seconds. Spread butter to cover plate.

3 . Pour egg mixture into pie plate. Microwave, covered with plastic wrap, on HIGH for 2 minutes.

4 . Tilt plate to move cooked egg toward center. Microwave, covered, on HIGH for 1 to 2 minutes or until omelet is firm.

5 . Top with avocado, sour cream, tomato and salsa. Microwave, covered, on HIGH for 2 minutes.

6 . Add cheese. Microwave, covered, on HIGH for 2 minutes or until cheese is melted.

7 . Let stand, covered, 2 minutes.

Serves 2 to 4.

Italian Omelet

4 eggs
4 tablespoons water or
  milk
½ teaspoon salt
⅛ teaspoon pepper
1 tablespoon butter or
  margarine

½ cup Mozzarella
  cheese, shredded
½ cup tomato sauce
1 teaspoon oregano
  leaves
1 tablespoon Parmesan
  cheese, grated

1. In a medium bowl, combine eggs, water, salt and pepper. Beat eggs well.

2. In a 9-inch pie plate, place butter, Microwave on HIGH for 30 seconds. Spread butter to cover plate.

3. Pour egg mixture into pie plate. Microwave, covered with plastic wrap, on HIGH for 2 minutes.

4. Tilt plate to move cooked eggs toward center. Microwave, covered, on HIGH for 1 to 2 minutes or until omelet is firm.

5. Top with Mozzarella cheese. Pour tomato sauce over cheese. Sprinkle with oregano and Parmesan cheese.

6. Microwave, covered, on HIGH for 3 to 4 minutes or until cheese is melted.

7. Let stand, covered, 2 minutes.

Serves 2 to 4.

A.M. - P.M. Mini-Quiche

½ pound ground beef
1 teaspoon MICRO
   SHAKE - Meat Flavor
1 cup milk
6 eggs

1 cup Cheddar cheese,
   shredded
½ teaspoon salt
½ teaspoon pepper
Paprika

1 . In a colander with drip pan, crumble hamburger. Sprinkle with MICRO SHAKE. Microwave on HIGH for 2 minutes. Stir to break up.

2 . In a small bowl, place milk. Microwave on HIGH for 1½ minutes.

3 . In a medium bowl, beat eggs. Add cheese, salt and pepper. Mix well.

4 . Stir in hot milk and finely crumbled ground beef.

5 . Into 6 custard cups, pour mixture.

6 . Microwave on HIGH for 7 to 8 minutes.

7 . Let stand 2 minutes. Sprinkle with paprika.

Serves 4 to 6.

NOTES _____

_____

_____

_____

_____

_____

_____

_____

Pork Sausage Quiche

1 9-inch frozen pie
  crust
6 ounces ground pork
  sausage (mild)
1 4-ounce can sliced
  mushrooms, drained

½ cup onion, chopped
2 tablespoons butter or
  margarine
3 eggs
1 cup sour cream

1 .   Transfer frozen pie crust into a 9-inch glass pie plate. Prick
       four times with a fork. Microwave on HIGH for 4 minutes.

2 .   On a roasting rack, crumble pork sausage. Microwave, covered
       with paper towel, on HIGH for 4 minutes.

3 .   In a small bowl, combine mushrooms, onion and butter.
       Microwave, covered, on HIGH for 5 minutes or until tender.

4 .   In a medium mixing bowl, beat eggs well. Add sour cream,
       sausage and mushroom mixture. Mix well. Pour into prepared
       pie crust. Microwave on MEDIUM for 15 to 17 minutes or un-
       til center is almost set.

5 .   Let stand 5 to 10 minutes.

Serves 4 to 6.

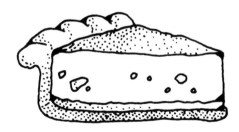

Crustless Zucchini Quiche

1 cup zucchini, shredded
½ cup sliced mushrooms
¼ cup onion, chopped
2 tablespoons butter or
　margarine
1 tablespoon MICRO
　SHAKE - Chicken
　Flavor

6 eggs
1 cup milk
½ teaspoon basil
¼ teaspoon pepper
1 cup Cheddar cheese,
　shredded

1 . In a 2-quart bowl, combine zucchini, mushrooms, onion, butter and MICRO SHAKE. Microwave, covered, on HIGH for 3 minutes.

2 . In a 3-quart bowl, combine eggs, milk, basil and pepper. Beat well. Stir in cooked vegetables and cheese.

3 . Into a 10-inch quiche dish or pie plate, pour mixture. Microwave on HIGH for 15 to 18 minutes or until center is almost set.

4 . Let stand 5 minutes.

Serves 4 to 6.

NOTES _____

_____

_____

_____

_____

_____

_____

_____

_____

Real Man's Quiche

6 strips bacon
1 13-ounce can
   evaporated milk
6 eggs

¼ teaspoon pepper
¼ teaspoon nutmeg
1½ cups Swiss cheese,
   shredded

1 . On a baking rack, place bacon. Microwave, covered with paper towel, on HIGH for 4 to 6 minutes or until crisp. Crumble and set aside.

2 . In a small bowl, place milk. Microwave on HIGH for 2½ minutes.

3 . In a medium mixing bowl, beat eggs. Add pepper, nutmeg and cheese. Stir well.

4 . Stir in hot milk and bacon bits. In a 9-inch quiche dish or pie plate, pour egg mixture. Microwave on HIGH for 10 to 12 minutes or until center is almost set.

5 . Let stand 5 minutes.

Serves 4 to 6.

Baba's Beef & Eggs

¼ cup onion, chopped
½ pound ground beef
MICRO SHAKE - Meat
   Flavor

1½ tablespoons fresh
   parsley, chopped
2 eggs
½ fresh lemon

1 . In a 2-quart casserole, combine onion and ground beef. Sprinkle with 1 teaspoon MICRO SHAKE.

2 . Microwave, covered, on HIGH for 2 minutes.

3 . Stir and continue microwaving for an additional 1 minute.

4 . Sprinkle parsley over meat. Distribute meat and form two openings for eggs. Crack eggs into openings. Squeeze fresh lemon juice over all.

5 . Microwave on HIGH for 2 to 3 minutes or until eggs are desired degree of doneness.

6 . Let stand 2 minutes.

Serves 2.

Hamburger Pie

½ pound lean ground
  beef
1 teaspoon MICRO
  SHAKE - Meat Flavor
4 eggs
½ cup green onion,
  sliced

⅓ cup milk
⅓ cup mayonnaise
½ teaspoon dill weed
¾ cup Cheddar cheese,
  shredded

1 . In a colander with drip pan, crumble ground beef. Sprinkle with MICRO SHAKE. Microwave on HIGH for 2 minutes. Stir to break up.

2 . In a small bowl, combine eggs, green onion, milk, mayonnaise and dill weed. Mix well. Add cooked ground beef.

3 . In a 9-inch pie plate or quiche dish, pour mixture.

4 . Microwave, covered with wax paper, on MEDIUM HIGH for 12 to 14 minutes or until egg is almost set.

5 . Cover pie with cheese. Microwave on MEDIUM for 1½ to 2 minutes or until cheese melts.

6 . Let stand, covered, 1 to 2 minutes.

Serve 4 to 6.

Desserts

Carrot Cake

3 eggs
1 ¼ cups sugar
1 cup oil
1 teaspoon vanilla
1 ½ cups all-purpose
flour
¾ teaspoon salt

1 ¼ teaspoons baking
soda
2 ½ teaspoons ground
cinnamon
2 ½ cups carrot, grated
1 cup pecans, chopped

1 . In a large mixing bowl, beat eggs. Add sugar, oil and vanilla. Mix well.

2 . In a small bowl, combine flour, salt, baking soda and cinnamon. Mix well.

3 . Stir flour mixture into egg mixture. Stir in carrots and nuts. Mix well.

4 . Grease a 12-cup ring mold. Pour batter into pan.

5 . Microwave on HIGH for 12 to 14 minutes or until cake pulls away from sides of pan.

6 . Invert immediately onto a serving platter. Cool and ice with cream cheese frosting.

Cream Cheese Frosting

1 pound box
confectioners sugar
1 8-ounce package
cream cheese

6 tablespoons butter or
margarine
2 teaspoons vanilla

1 . In a medium mixing bowl, place sugar. Add cream cheese and butter.

2 . Microwave on HIGH for 1 minute. Mix well. Add vanilla. Beat with a fork until fluffy.

Apple Raisin Cake

6 tablespoons all-purpose flour
4 tablespoons whole wheat flour
1 cup sugar
1 teaspoon baking soda
½ teaspoon salt
½ teaspoon ground cinnamon
¼ teaspoon ground cloves
¼ teaspoon ground nutmeg
⅛ teaspoon allspice
1 egg
¼ cup vegetable oil
2 baking apples, peeled and finely chopped
3 tablespoons raisins
¼ cup pecans, chopped

1 . In a medium mixing bowl, combine first nine dry ingredients. Mix well.

2 . In a large mixing bowl, beat egg and oil. Add dry ingredients and mix thoroughly.

3 . Add apples, raisins and nuts. Stir well.

4 . Pour batter into a greased 8 × 8 baking dish.

5 . Microwave on HIGH for 8 minutes or until cake pulls away from sides of pan. Center will appear slightly moist. This will firm as it cools. Ice with Frosting.

Frosting

2 tablespoons butter or margarine
4 tablespoons brown sugar
1 tablespoon milk
½ cup confectioners sugar
¼ teaspoon vanilla

1 . In a small mixing bowl, place butter. Microwave on HIGH for 30 seconds. Add brown sugar and milk.

2 . Microwave on HIGH for 1 minute. Stir. Microwave on HIGH for 30 seconds. Stir well. Allow to cool for 15 to 30 minutes.

3 . When lukewarm, beat in confectioners sugar and vanilla. Add 1 tablespoon milk if necessary or thicken with additional sugar for good spreading consistency.

Yield: 16 2-inch squares

Lemonade Cake

½ cup graham cracker
  crumbs
1 6-ounce can frozen
  lemonade concentrate,
  thawed
1 18½-ounce yellow
  cake mix

1 3⅛-ounce package
  instant vanilla pudding
  mix
½ cup vegetable oil
4 eggs

Glaze

1 cup confectioners sugar
½ teaspoon lemon peel
2 teaspoons butter, melted
milk

1 . Lightly grease a 12-cup ring mold. Sprinkle graham cracker crumbs into pan; coat thoroughly.

2 . In a small bowl, pour lemonade concentrate. Microwave on HIGH for 1 minute. Remove 2 teaspoons of concentrate and reserve for glaze.

3 . In a large mixing bowl, combine cake and pudding mixes, oil, eggs and lemonade concentrate. Blend well. Pour into prepared pan.

4 . Microwave on HIGH for 12 minutes or until cake pulls away from the edges.

5 . Invert immediately onto serving platter.

6 . To prepare glaze; combine reserved lemonade concentrate, confectioners sugar, lemon peel and butter. Blend well. Add milk until mixture reaches desired consistency. Beat until smooth. Drizzle over cooled cake.

Serves 12 to 16.

Chocolate Chip Cake

Topping

¼ cup butter or margarine
2 tablespoons brown sugar
⅔ cup pecans, finely chopped

Cake

2¾ cups all-purpose
flour
2 teaspoons baking
soda
1 teaspoon salt
1 tablespoon vinegar
7 tablespoons whole
milk

1 cup butter or
margarine
1 cup brown sugar
1 tablespoon vanilla
4 eggs
1 12-ounce package
semi-sweet
chocolate morsels

1 . In a small bowl, place ¼ cup butter. Microwave on HIGH for
30 seconds to soften. Add brown sugar and pecans. Stir until
crumbly.

2 . Grease a 12-cup ring mold with oil. Spoon pecan mixture into
bottom of ring mold. Press to cover entire bottom of pan.

3 . In a small bowl, combine flour, baking soda and salt. Set aside.

4 . Place vinegar and milk in a 1-cup liquid measure. Set aside.

5 . In a large mixing bowl, place butter. Microwave on HIGH for
30 seconds. Add brown sugar and vanilla. Beat at medium
speed until light and fluffy. Add eggs, one at a time, beating
well after each addition. Turn mixer to low.

6 . Gradually add flour mixture, one third at a time, alternating
with milk. Gently fold in semi-sweet morsels with a rubber
spatula.

7 . Pour into prepared pan. Microwave on HIGH for 12 to 14
minutes or until cake pulls away from sides of pan.

Pumpkin Cheesecake

6 tablespoons butter or margarine
1½ cups crushed graham crackers
1 cup sugar
4 3-ounce packages cream cheese
1½ teaspoons flour
¾ teaspoon lemon peel, grated
¾ teaspoon orange peel, grated
3 eggs
1 cup canned pumpkin
1 teaspoon vanilla
1 cup sour cream

1. In a 9-inch pie plate, place butter. Microwave on HIGH for 1 minute. Add crackers and 2 tablespoons sugar to melted butter. Combine ingredients and press firmly to form a crust. Microwave on HIGH for 2 minutes. Set aside.

2. In a medium mixing bowl, place cream cheese. Microwave on HIGH for 1½ minutes. Stir well. Add ¾ cup sugar, flour, lemon peel, orange peel, eggs, pumpkin and ½ teaspoon vanilla. Beat until smooth.

3. Microwave on HIGH for 4 minutes, stirring every minute. Pour cheese mixture into prepared crust.

4. Microwave on HIGH for 4 minutes or until puffed around the edges. Let stand for 5 minutes.

5. In a small bowl, combine sour cream, 2 tablespoons sugar and ½ teaspoon vanilla. Spread over top of cake. Microwave on HIGH for 2 minutes.

6. Let stand for 5 minutes. Refrigerate before serving.

Serves 6.

Zucchini Cake

3 eggs
2 cups sugar
1 cup oil
2 cups zucchini, grated
2 cups all-purpose flour
1½ teaspoon baking
soda

1 teaspoon salt
3 teaspoons ground
cinnamon
2 teaspoons vanilla
1 cup pecans, chopped

1 . In a large mixing bowl, beat eggs. Add sugar and oil. Mix well.
2 . In a small bowl, combine flour, baking soda, salt and cinnamon. Mix well. Add to above mixture and mix well. Add zucchini, vanilla and nuts. Mix well.
3 . Grease a 12-cup ring mold. Pour batter into pan.
4 . Microwave on HIGH for 12 to 14 minutes or until cake pulls away from sides of pan.
5 . Invert immediately onto a serving platter. Cool and ice with cream cheese frosting (see Carrot Cake Frosting).

Quick Cheesecake

6 tablespoons butter or
margarine
1½ cups crushed graham
crackers
9 tablespoons sugar
1 8-ounce package cream
cheese

1 egg
1 tablespoon lemon
juice
1 tablespoon lemon peel,
grated
1 cup sour cream

1 . In a 9-inch pie plate, place butter. Microwave on HIGH for 1 minute. Add crackers and 2 tablespoons sugar. Combine ingredients and press firmly to form a crust. Microwave on HIGH for 2 minutes. Set aside.

2 . In a small bowl, place cream cheese. Microwave on HIGH for 45 seconds. Add egg, lemon juice, lemon peel and 5 tablespoons sugar. Beat until smooth.

3 . Pour cheese mixture into prepared crust. Microwave on HIGH for 5 minutes. Let stand for 5 minutes.

4 . Combine sour cream and 3 tablespoons sugar. Spread over top of cake. Microwave on HIGH for 2 minutes.

5 . Let stand for 5 minutes. Refrigerate before serving.

Serves 6.

Carnival Caramel Corn

7 large marshmallows
½ cup butter or
  margarine
  (do not use soft-type
  margarine)

½ cup brown sugar
2 to 3 quarts popped
  popcorn

1 . In a large bowl, combine marshmallows, butter and brown
    sugar. Microwave on HIGH for 2½ minutes. Stir well until
    blended. Microwave an additional 30 seconds or until
    marshmallows are melted. Stir again.

2 . Place popcorn in a large, buttered pan. Pour caramel mixture
    over and toss to coat evenly.

3 . Pour coated corn on wax paper and let it cool.

Yield: 2 to 3 quarts.

Peanut Popcorn Balls

1 14-ounce package light
  caramels
3 tablespoons water
1 tablespoon butter or
  margarine

2 to 3 quarts popped
  popcorn
1½ cups Spanish peanuts

1 . In a small mixing bowl, combine caramels, water and butter.
    Microwave on MEDIUM for 5 to 6 minutes or until melted.
    Stir 1 to 2 times during heating.

2 . In a large mixing bowl, combine popcorn and nuts. Pour
    caramel mixture over and toss to coat evenly.

3 . Grease or moisten hands and form into balls.

4 . Place popcorn balls on waxed paper to set.

Easy Chocolate Mousse

1 6-ounce package semi-
  sweet chocolate
  morsels
1 cup milk

¼ cup sugar
1 tablespoon Kaluha
Whipped cream, optional
4 eggs

1 . In a small bowl, place chocolate morsels. Microwave on HIGH
     for 2 minutes or until melted.

2 . In a small bowl, place milk. Microwave on HIGH for 1
     minute.

3 . In a blender, place chocolate, milk, eggs, sugar and Kaluha.
     Blend 1 minute.

4 . Pour into custard cups. Refrigerate overnight.

5 . Garnish with whipped cream before serving.

Serves 4.

Caramel Pecan Dream Bars

⅓ cup butter or
  margarine
1 18½-ounce package
  yellow cake mix
2 eggs
1 14-ounce can sweet-
  ened condensed milk

1 teaspoon vanilla
1 cup pecans, chopped
½ cup almond brickle
  baking chips

1 . In a large mixing bowl, place butter. Microwave on HIGH
     for 30 seconds just to soften.

2 . Add cake mix and 1 egg to softened butter. Mix well on
     high speed of hand mixer until crumbly.

3 . Press mixture into a greased 2-quart oblong baking dish.

4 . In a small bowl, beat milk, egg and vanilla until well
     blended. Stir in pecans and almond brickle chips. Pour
     over base; spread to cover evenly.

5 . Microwave on MEDIUM HIGH for 14 to 16 minutes or
     until center is almost set. Allow bars to cool completely
     before cutting into 2-inch squares.

Yield: 35 2-inch squares.

Turtle Brownies

1 14-ounce package caramels
⅔ cup evaporated milk
1 18½-ounce box German chocolate cake mix

¾ cup butter or margarine, softened
1 cup nuts, chopped
1 12-ounce package semi-sweet chocolate morsels

1. In a small mixing bowl, combine caramels and ⅓ cup milk.

2. Microwave on HIGH for 4 minutes or until melted.

3. In a mixing bowl, combine cake mix, remaining milk and butter. Mix until mixture holds together. Stir in nuts. Press half of cake mix into a greased 2-quart oblong baking dish.

4. Microwave on HIGH for 4 minutes.

5. Sprinkle one-half of chocolate morsels evenly on top. Pour melted caramels over mixture. Crumble remaining cake mixture on top or caramels and top with remaining chocolate morsels.

6. Microwave on HIGH for 15 to 18 minutes or until center is set.

7. Let stand until cooled. Cut into 2-inch squares.

Makes 35 2-inch squares.

Hot Apple Crisp

6 cooking apples, thinly
  sliced
1 tablespoon lemon juice
¼ cup all-purpose flour
2½ teaspoons cinnamon
⅔ cup bisquick

⅔ cup brown sugar
4 tablespoons butter or
  margarine
1 cup pecans, chopped

1. In a 2-quart shallow baking dish, place apples. Sprinkle with lemon juice. Add ¼ cup flour, 1½ teaspoons cinnamon. Toss well to coat apples

2. In a small mixing bowl, combine bisquick, brown sugar, butter, pecans and 1 teaspoon cinnamon.

3. Sprinkle on top of apple mixture.

4. Microwave on HIGH for 10 to 12 minutes or until apples are tender. Serve hot.

Serves 6.

Almond Butter Toffee

Butter for greasing
  utensils
½ cup butter or
  margarine
1 cup granulated sugar
½ teaspoon salt

¼ cup water
1 4-ounce package sliced
  almonds
1 4-ounce milk chocolate
  bar

1. Butter a large, deep bowl along the top edge. Place ½ cup butter in the bowl. Pour sugar directly on butter; avoid getting sugar on sides of bowl. Add salt and water.

2. Microwave on HIGH for 7 minutes. Continue microwaving in 30 second intervals until light brown.

3. Place almonds on a buttered cookie sheet. Pour prepared mixture over almonds. Allow to cool.

4. In a small bowl, place chocolate bar. Microwave on HIGH for 1½ minutes. Spread melted chocolate over candy. Allow to cool. Refrigerate before breaking into pieces.

Beverages

HOUSE SPECIAL

Eggnog

4 cups milk
6 egg yolks
½ cup sugar

¼ teaspoon nutmeg
¼ teaspoon cinnamon
¼ teaspoon vanilla

1 . Pour milk into a 2-quart deep casserole. Microwave on HIGH for 5 minutes.

2 . In a medium mixing bowl, beat egg yolks with sugar. Add nutmeg, cinnamon and vanilla.

3 . Stir 1 cup hot milk into egg mixture. Then, blend egg mixture into milk. Microwave on HIGH for 5 minutes or until hot and bubbly. Serve hot or refrigerate and serve cold.

Makes: 1 quart

Espresso Au Lait

4 ounces milk
4 ounces Espresso, brewed
Sugar, optional

1 .   In a small cup, place milk. Microwave on HIGH for 45 seconds.

2 .   Divide espresso into two cups. Add milk dividing evenly. Stir. Add sugar if desired.

Serves 2

Coffee de Cacao

24 ounces coffee,
  microwave brewed
2 ounces Creme de
  Cacao

2 ounces white Creme
  de Menthe
1 cup light cream
Coffee ice cubes

1 .   In a blender, place cooled coffee, liqueurs and light cream. Blend until frothy.

2 .   Serve over coffee ice cubes.

Serves 4 to 6.

Irish Coffee

2 lemon wedges
⅓ cup granulated white
  sugar
6 ounces Irish whiskey

24 ounces coffee
  microwave brewed
Whipped cream

1 .   Rub wedge of lemon around the rim of 4 Irish coffee mugs. Put granulated sugar in a small bowl. Press the rim of the mugs into the sugar. Let sugar dry slightly.

2 .   Put 1 teaspoon sugar in each mug. Add 1½ ounces Irish whiskey and 6 ounces coffee.

3 .   Serve garnished with whipped cream.

Serves 4.

Moonlight Cappucino

2 teaspoons honey
½ teaspoon vanilla
½ teaspoon cocoa
  powder
½ cup milk

4 ounces Espresso,
  brewed
2 cinnamon sticks
Chocolate, grated

1 . In a 1-cup measure, combine honey, vanilla, cocoa and milk. Microwave on HIGH for 1 to 1½ minutes or until hot. Stir to blend ingredients. Whip with a wire whisk until frothy.

2 . Fill tall thin cups ⅓ full with hot milk, then tilt each cup and pour coffee down the side until full.

3 . Serve with a cinnamon stick and top with grated chocolate.

Serves 2.

Hot Chocolate

1 square unsweetened
  chocolate
½ cup water
1½ tablespoons sugar

1½ cups milk
Whipped cream, optional

1 . In a 1-quart deep mixing bowl, place chocolate and water. Microwave on HIGH for 1½ minutes. Stir well.

2 . Add sugar. Microwave on HIGH for 1 minute.

3 . Gradually add milk, stirring constantly.

4 . Microwave on HIGH for 2 minutes. Stir. Beat with rotary beater or hand mixer.

5 . Serve garnished with whipped cream.

Serves 2.

Cranapple Punch

1 quart apple cider
3 cups cranberry juice
   cocktail
2 tablespoons brown
   sugar

3 sticks cinnamon
½ teaspoon whole
   cloves
½ lemon, thinly sliced

1 . In a 3-quart deep bowl, combine ingredients.

2 . Microwave on HIGH for 10 minutes.

3 . Before serving, remove spices with a slotted spoon.

Serves 8.

Fruit Tea Punch

1 cup water
2 black tea bags
2 tablespoons lemon
   juice
1 cup orange juice
1 10-ounce package
   frozen strawberries,
   thawed

2 cups club soda
1 lemon, sliced
1 orange, sliced

1 . Place water and tea bags in a measuring cup. Microwave on HIGH for 3 minutes. Remove tea bags.

2 . In a 2-quart deep mixing bowl, combine tea with lemon juice, orange juice and strawberries. Cover and refrigerate.

3 . When ready to serve, add club soda. Garnish with slices of orange and lemon.

Serves 8.

Childrens

Nutritious Granola

1½ cups quick oats, uncooked

½ cup coconut, flaked

½ cup pecans, coarsely chopped

2 tablespoons honey

1 tablespoon butter or margarine, melted

¾ teaspoon ground cinnamon

½ cup raisins

1. In a 9-inch shallow baking dish, combine all ingredients except raisins. Stir well.

2. Microwave on HIGH for 4 minutes, stirring twice.

3. Microwave for 1 to 3 minutes or until golden brown.
   Stir well.

4. Add raisins. Stir well. Cool

Makes 2½ cups.

Speedy Hot Chocolate

¾ cup milk
1 tablespoon chocolate syrup

1. Place milk in a mug. Stir in chocolate. Blend well.

2. Microwave on HIGH for 1 to 1½ minutes or until desired degree of serving temperature.

Serves 1.

Adam's Teething Biscuit

1 egg
3 tablespoons oil
3 tablespoons sugar
½ cup dark molasses
1 tablespoon vinegar
½ teaspoon baking soda

2 to 2½ cups all-
   purpose flour
2 tablespoons wheat
   germ

1. In a medium mixing bowl, beat egg. Add oil and sugar. Stir well.

2. Beat in molasses and vinegar.

3. In a small bowl, combine remaining ingredients.

4. Stir dry ingredients into egg mixture ½ cup at a time, until evenly mixed.

5. Chill dough for at least 2 hours.

6. Pinch off a small amount of dough. Roll ⅛-inch thick on lightly floured wax paper. Cut dough into 2×3-inch rectangles. Slide sheet of cardboard underneath wax paper.

7. Microwave on HIGH for 1½ minutes for 2 biscuits. If bubbles occur, pierce with pin so air can escape.

Makes: 16 biscuits.

Hamburgers

1 pound lean ground beef
MICRO SHAKE - Meat Flavor

1 . Form ground beef into 4 patties.

2 . When ready for one hamburger, moisten both sides of each patty with water. Sprinkle liberally with MICRO SHAKE to cover both sides. Place on a plate.

3 . Microwave, covered, on HIGH for 1½ minutes or until desired degree of doneness.

Serves 4.

Meatball Snack

lean ground beef
MICRO SHAKE - Meat Flavor

1 . Form 1-inch meatballs.

2 . Place 2 meatballs on a paper plate. Sprinkle liberally with MICRO SHAKE to cover all sides.

3 . Microwave, covered, on HIGH for 45 seconds. Eat with a toothpick. Make as many as you need.

Crackers & Cheese

8 crackers
salsa, catsup or barbecue sauce
Cheddar cheese, grated

1 . On a dinner plate or paper plate, place crackers. Top each cracker with favorite sauce. Sprinkle Cheddar cheese on each cracker.

2 . Microwave, covered, on HIGH for 30 seconds or until cheese is melted.

Serves 1.

Scrambled Eggs

2 eggs
1 tablespoon water or milk
2 tablespoons Cheddar cheese, grated

1 . In a small serving bowl, crack eggs. Beat eggs with a fork. Add milk and continue beating.

2 . Microwave on HIGH for 1 minute. Stir well to break up outer edge of cooked egg.

3 . Microwave on HIGH for 30 seconds. Stir well. Add cheese.

4 . Microwave on HIGH for 30 seconds or until cheese in melted. Salt and pepper to taste.

Serves 1.

Easy Fried Egg

½ teaspoon butter or margarine
1 egg
1 slice Cheddar cheese

1 . In a small serving bowl, place butter. Microwave on HIGH for 20 to 30 seconds or until melted.

2 . Break egg into melted butter. Prick yolk with a fork.

3 . Microwave on HIGH for 45 to 60 seconds.

4 . Add slice of cheese. Microwave on HIGH for 30 seconds or until cheese is melted. Salt and pepper to taste.

Serves 1.

S'Mores

2 graham cracker squares
1 regular size marshmallow
4 small squares milk chocolate bar

1 . On a small plate or napkin, place graham cracker. Place squares of chocolate on cracker. Place marshmallow on top of chocolate.

2 . Microwave on HIGH for 20 to 30 seconds or until melted.

3 . Top with another graham cracker.

Serves 1.

Baked Apple

1 baking apple
1 teaspoon raisins
1 teaspoon brown sugar

Dash ground cinnamon
½ teaspoon butter or
margarine

1 . Wash and core apple. Slice off a thin circle of peel about ½-inch from top of apple

2 . In a small bowl or custard cup, place apple. Place raisins and brown sugar in cavity of apple. Sprinkle with cinnamon. Top with butter.

3 . Microwave, covered, for 2 minutes.

4 . Let stand, covered, for 2 minutes before eating.

Serves 1.

Chocolate Corn Flakes Treat

1 8-ounce milk chocolate bar
3 to 3½ cups corn flakes
½ cup raisins

1 . In a large mixing bowl, place chocolate. Microwave on HIGH for 1 to 1½ minutes or until melted. Stir well.

2 . Add corn flakes. Mix well. Toss raisins in mixture. Mix well.

3 . Drop by spoonfuls on greased cookie sheet. Let harden in refrigerator.

Makes 24 treats.

Crunchy Fudge Squares

1 6-ounce package butterscotch morsels
½ cup peanut butter
4 cups rice krispies
1 6-ounce package semi-sweet chocolate morsels

1 tablespoon water
½ cup confectioners sugar
2 tablespoons butter or margarine

1 . In a large mixing bowl, place butterscotch morsels and peanut butter. Microwave on HIGH for 1 minute. Stir well.

2 . Gradually add rice krispies to melted peanut butter mixture. Stir well.

3 . Press half of mixture into a greased 8 × 8 square baking dish. Chill in refrigerator.

4 . In a small bowl, place semi-sweet chocolate, water, sugar and butter. Microwave on HIGH for 1 minute. Stir well.

5 . Pour melted chocolate over rice krispies. Spread remaining rice krispies over chocolate. Press gently. Chill, cut into squares.

Makes 25 1½-inch squares.

Fort Wayne Snow Ice Cream

½ cup milk
2 eggs
½ cup sugar

½ teaspoon vanilla
1 gallon fresh snow

1 . In a small bowl, place milk. Microwave on HIGH for 1 to 2 minutes or until bubbles appear around edges.

2 . In a 3-quart deep bowl, beat eggs slightly. Add sugar and vanilla. Slowly add warm milk. Stir well.

3 . Add snow gradually to mixture. Stir until mushy.

Yield: 1 gallon

Pumpkin Compote

1 small pumpkin
4 cooking apples, cored
   and cubed
½ cup brown sugar
4 tablespoons butter or
   margarine

1 cup pecans, chopped
1 cup raisins
1 cup coconut, flaked
1 teaspoon ground
   cinnamon

1 . Remove top portion of pumpkin. Clean out inner membranes of pumpkin and seeds.

2 . Place remaining ingredients in cavity of pumpkin.

3 . Microwave, covered tightly with plastic wrap, on HIGH for 10 to 15 minutes or until apples are tender. Serve hot over ice cream.

Serves 8.

Banana Coconut Pudding

1 3⅝-ounce package
vanilla pudding and
pie filling mix, cook
variety

2 cups milk
1 banana, sliced
2 teaspoons coconut,
flaked

1 . In a medium mixing bowl, combine pudding and milk.

2 . Microwave on HIGH for 3 minutes. Stir. Continue microwaving on HIGH for 1 to 3 minutes or until thick.

3 . Stir in bananas.

4 . Pour into custard cups. Sprinkle ½ teaspoon coconut on top.

Serves 4.

Banana Sandwich

1 tablespoon peanut
butter
1 tablespoon butter or
margarine, softened
1 tablespoon brown
sugar

1 tablespoon pecans,
chopped
1 banana

1 . In a small bowl, combine first four ingredients. Stir well until smooth.

2 . Cut banana in half lengthwise. Place on a small plate. Spread peanut butter mixture over banana slices.

3 . Microwave, covered, on HIGH for 1 minute.

Serves 1.

Index

NOTES

THE MICRO SHAKE GIFT
End Microwave Browning Problems

Order MICRO SHAKE set(s) from:
MICRO SHAKE Foods, Inc.
P.O. Box 53
Malibu, CA 90265

- ✂

ORIGINAL MICRO SHAKE FLAVORS
(Select three shakers of your choice)

No. of Shakers

Char Brown Natural Meat Flavor   _____
Char Brown Meat with Onion & Garlic Flavor   _____
Natural Chicken Country Fried Flavor   _____

Three-shaker set at $7.99
(includes postage & handling)

SALT FREE MICRO SHAKE FLAVORS
(Select two shakers of your choice)

No. of Shakers

Salt Free Meat Flavor   _____
Salt Free Chicken Flavor   _____

Two-shaker set at $6.99
(includes postage & handling)

See other side for order information.
Allow 4 of 6 weeks for delivery.

- -

ORIGINAL MICRO SHAKE FLAVORS
(Select three shakers of your choice)

No. of Shakers

Char Brown Natural Meat Flavor   _____
Char Brown Meat with Onion & Garlic Flavor   _____
Natural Chicken Country Fried Flavor   _____

Three-shaker set at $7.99
(includes postage & handling)

SALT FREE MICRO SHAKE FLAVORS
(Select two shakers of your choice)

No. of Shakers

Salt Free Meat Flavor   _____
Salt Free Chicken Flavor   _____

Two-shaker set at $6.99
(includes postage & handling)

See other side for order information.
Allow 4 of 6 weeks for delivery.

Please send MICRO SHAKE set(s) to:

Name _____

Address _____

City _____ State _____ Zip _____

My check/money order, payable to MICRO SHAKE Foods, Inc., for $_____
is enclosed.

Please include card to read: "This MICRO SHAKE set is sent to you with the
compliments of _____."

Please send MICRO SHAKE set(s) to:

Name _____

Address _____

City_____ State_____ Zip_____

My check/money order, payable to MICRO SHAKE Foods, Inc., for $_____
is enclosed.

Please include card to read: "This MICRO SHAKE set is sent to you with the
compliments of _____."

"FANTASTIC FOOD FROM YOUR MICROWAVE"
The Perfect Gift for Friends and Relatives

Use the order forms below to have copies of "FANTASTIC FOOD FROM YOUR MICROWAVE" sent to a friend or relative as a gift. Send $7.95 plus $1.50 for shipping & handling (per copy) to:

MICRO SHAKE Foods, Inc.
P.O. Box 53
Malibu, CA 90265

*Allow 4 to 6 weeks for delivery.

Please send _____ copies of FANTASTIC FOOD FROM YOUR MICROWAVE to:

Name _____

Address _____

City _____ State _____ Zip _____

My check/money order payable to Micro Shake Foods, Inc., for $ _____ ($9.45 per copy, includes postage and handling) is enclosed. (California residents add 6.5% sales tax)

Please include card to read: "FANTASTIC FOOD FROM YOUR MICROWAVE is sent to you with the compliments of _____."

Please send _____ copies of FANTASTIC FOOD FROM YOUR MICROWAVE to:

Name _____

Address _____

City _____ State _____ Zip _____

My check/money order payable to Micro Shake Foods, Inc., for $ _____ ($9.45 per copy, includes postage and handling) is enclosed. (California residents add 6.5% sales tax)

Please include card to read: "FANTASTIC FOOD FROM YOUR MICROWAVE is sent to you with the compliments of _____."

I know someone who would find MICRO SHAKE and/or "Fantastic Food From Your Microwave" to be a great asset for their microwave cooking. Please send recipes and order form to:

NAME _____

ADDRESS_____

CITY _____ STATE _____ ZIP _____

I know someone who would find MICRO SHAKE and/or "Fantastic Food From Your Microwave" to be a great asset for their microwave cooking. Please send recipes and order form to:

NAME _____

ADDRESS_____

CITY _____ STATE _____ ZIP _____